J. M. Barrie's *Peter Pan*

'Do you believe in fairies? Say quick that you believe!'
– Peter Pan

Peter Pan is a narrative many of us believe we know well, and yet the J.M. Barrie play that premiered on a West End stage in December 1904 is not the depiction of Peter, Wendy, Hook, and Never Land that most people have experienced. It was the critical and commercial success of this particular play which propelled the notoriety and appeal of the story, and without the success of that first production, *Peter Pan* would not be such a familiar part of our mainstream culture. Lucie Sutherland examines how, and why, this play became so popular, why the trans-Atlantic collaboration of Barrie and Charles Frohman was vital to the success of the 1904 production, and how key versions in England and America have created an iconic narrative that remains popular today.

This book charts the 'awfully big adventure' of creating *Peter Pan*, as well as the many entertaining, enthralling, and often extraordinary ways the play has been adapted ever since.

Lucie Sutherland is Assistant Professor in Drama at the University of Nottingham, UK.

The Fourth Wall

The Fourth Wall series is a growing collection of short books on famous plays. Its compact format perfectly suits the kind of fresh, engaging criticism that brings a play to life.

Each book in this series selects one play or musical as its subject and approaches it from an original angle, seeking to shed light on an old favourite or break new ground on a modern classic. These lively, digestible books are a must for anyone looking for new ideas on the major works of modern theatre.

www.routledge.com/performance/series/4THW

Also available in this series:

J. M. Synge's *The Playboy of the Western World* by Christopher Collins
Heiner Müller's *The Hamletmachine* by David Barnett
Lerner and Loewe's *My Fair Lady* by Keith Garebian
Samuel Beckett's *Krapp's Last Tape* by Daniel Sack
Thornton Wilder's *The Skin of Our Teeth* by Kyle Gillette
Harold Pinter's *Party Time* by Graham White
Davies and Penhall's *Sunny Afternoon* by John Fleming
Tim Crouch's *An Oak Tree* by Catherine Love
Sondheim and Lapine's *Into the Woods* by Olaf Jubin
Errol John's *Moon on a Rainbow Shawl* by Lynnette Goddard
Alastair McDowell's *Pomona* by David Ian Rabey
Benjamin Britten's *Peter Grimes* by Sam Kinchin-Smith
Sondheim and Wheeler's *Sweeney Todd* by Aaron Thomas
Edward Albee's *Who's Afraid of Virginia Woolf?* by Michael Y. Bennett
Boublil and Schoënberg's *Les Misérables* by Sarah Whitfield
J. M. Barrie's *Peter Pan* by Lucie Sutherland

J. M. Barrie's *Peter Pan*

Lucie Sutherland

Routledge
Taylor & Francis Group
LONDON AND NEW YORK

First published 2019
by Routledge
2 Park Square, Milton Park, Abingdon, Oxon OX14 4RN

and by Routledge
52 Vanderbilt Avenue, New York, NY 10017

Routledge is an imprint of the Taylor & Francis Group, an informa business

British Library Cataloguing-in-Publication Data
A catalogue record for this book is available from the British Library

Library of Congress Cataloging-in-Publication Data
A catalog record has been requested for this book

ISBN: 978-1-138-67888-0 (pbk)
ISBN: 978-1-315-55860-8 (ebk)

Typeset in Bembo
by Apex CoVantage, LLC

Dedicated to the memory of my father, Ian Sutherland.

Contents

Acknowledgements

My appreciation as always to the V & A staff at Blythe House who made my time working with items from the Theatre and Performance collections truly productive. Tremendous thanks also to Ben Piggott and Laura Soppelsa at Routledge for all their help and guidance.

Thank you to John Stokes, who first introduced me to *Peter Pan* as a text to be studied. I am also extremely grateful to Margaret D. Stetz and Victoria Ford Smith, who collaborated with me on an MLA panel a few years ago, confirming just how much there is to say about this play and about Barrie.

To every colleague, friend, and family member who has been so helpful and supportive, I am so grateful. I must also acknowledge the crucial part played by Milly and Molly in the completion of this book; their input is hard to describe, but it's here.

Particular thanks go to Sarah Davison for taking the time, as she always does, to be the most excellent friend; to Faith Evans, who continues to provide invaluable guidance, encouragement, and friendship; and to Rozelle Sutherland, MBE, for supporting me in this, as in everything. Special thanks as well to Peter Loftus as it was a privilege to talk to him about this play and its author, and to Dorothy Pearce, who remains an inspiration.

Finally, I dedicate this book to the memory of my father Ian Sutherland. He would have liked it very much, especially the film bits.

Introduction

This book explores the play, *Peter Pan*, first staged at the Duke of York's Theatre in London's West End on 27th December 1904. It is concerned with the development of the text, initial productions, and many subsequent incarnations: as pantomime, on film, in animation, and appropriated within popular culture through quotation and allusion.

Peter Pan has proved itself to be versatile drama. The play is regularly adapted, but that is not simply because its author, James Matthew Barrie, created a new fairy tale that brought pleasure to its audiences. Although *Peter Pan* is in many ways a light and often comic drama, developed and first staged as family entertainment at Christmas time, the play fuses its ethereal, otherworldly characters and environments with pathos, producing at times a melancholic, and even a dark, subtext. As Jacqueline Rose asserts, *Peter Pan* 'shows innocence not as a property of childhood but as a portion of adult desire', a longing for rather than a representation of children's experience and imagined worlds.[1] One reason for the enduring appeal of the play is its resistance to adult experience and behaviour. Peter is a boy who is happy not to grow up, happy to live apart from his mother, to battle anyone who might be a father-figure, and to experience death should the occasion arise. He is an individual who shows a disregard for several human concerns: time, affection, and memory. Therefore while many aspects of the play including its spectacle and dynamic action appeal to a young audience, this has never been a play that is simply or exclusively for children. Many later versions have jettisoned some of the most difficult material. For example, the 1953 Disney animation avoids references to death and mortality altogether. However, it is indisputable that some of the best-known lines from the play resonate with darker themes, notably: 'To die will be an awfully big adventure'.[2]

People producing, adapting, and researching the play now have to confront some challenging material; specifically, the language and attitudes found within *Peter Pan* that relate to colonialism, gender, and race. Some recent productions have remained faithful to Barrie's script, and have therefore come in for criticism, seen as promoting indefensible perspectives. Elizabeth Broadbent notes in relation to the depiction of First Nations characters: 'while the fantasy has long been protected by its intentions – the Indians are portrayed through the eyes of a child – it's time to confront the deep-seated problems with the story itself and even with modern portrayals'.[3] Significantly, the two most recent productions of the play by England's major, subsidised producing companies, the Royal Shakespeare Company (RSC) and the National Theatre (NT), substantially altered the text so that action is perceived from the point of view of the female characters. The RSC production (2013) was adapted by Ella Hickson who used both the published 1928 play text and *Peter and Wendy*, a prose version of the story first published by Barrie in 1911; Hickson framed the action in Never Land as Wendy's response to tension within her family.[4] In 2016 the NT, in a co-production with Bristol Old Vic authored 'by J.M. Barrie and the Companies', altered conventional casting and doubling practices for the play, with the actor playing Mrs. Darling also playing Captain Hook (the conventional practice is for one actor to play Mr. Darling and the pirate).[5] The necessity and the process of adapting Barrie's text will be examined in greater depth in Chapter 3, but it is important to begin by acknowledging the difficulties as well as the pleasures that are evident within this play.

In the following chapters the form and content of *Peter Pan* will be discussed and then attention will be paid to early productions in London and New York, and the theatre professionals associated with those productions who helped to shape the published text, before some later versions of the play – on stage and screen – are scrutinised. Both the published play that is available to be read and staged today, and its enduring influence, will be the focus. Arguably, next to Shakespeare, *Peter Pan* is the work of English drama most often adapted to speak to new and diverse audiences. Defining *Peter Pan* as English drama is a controversial act as its author was Scottish by birth. Yet Barrie wrote primarily for the English mainstream theatre; *Peter Pan* was written to be performed in London's West End, the heart of commercial theatre in the United Kingdom in 1904 (and still today). Before turning to the text and first productions, however, further information about the author will be helpful in explaining the origins of the play.

J.M. Barrie

Barrie spent most of his working life in London, writing journalism, fiction, and most famously drama. However, he was born on 9th May 1860 at Kirriemuir, Forfarshire, Scotland, to Margaret Ogilvy and handloom weaver David Barrie; he was the ninth of ten children. When Barrie was seven, an older brother (also David) was killed in a skating accident and the younger sibling spent a considerable amount of his childhood trying to combat his mother's grief by, for example, dressing in the clothes of his deceased brother and putting on a range of performances to both entertain and to reminisce about the lost boy; practices described by Barrie in the memoir *Margaret Ogilvy* (1896). This part of the author's life has often been linked to his eventual work as a dramatist, and in relation to *Peter Pan* specifically, these early experiences resonate in his creation of a part-human, part-supernatural boy who is a pervasive but ultimately elusive presence. The ghost of David Barrie has been identified with Peter by critics including Andrew Birkin:

> If Margaret Ogilvy drew a measure of comfort from the notion that David, in dying a boy, would remain a boy for ever, Barrie drew inspiration. It would be another thirty-three years before that inspiration emerged in the shape of Peter Pan, but here was the germ, rooted in his mind and soul from the age of six.[6]

While the relationship with his mother was a defining part of his childhood and early adolescence, Barrie was also taking part in formal education that prepared the way for a career as a writer. From 1868 he was in full time education, attending the Glasgow Academy, then the Forfar Academy, before enrolling at Edinburgh University in 1878, and graduating in 1882 with an MA level degree. By March 1883, Barrie was a leader writer with the *Nottingham Journal*, and by March 1885, he was a freelance journalist in London and was working in earnest as a novelist. It is also worth noting that as early as 1877, while still at Forfar Academy, he had a play, *Bandelero the Bandit*, staged by the Dumfries Amateur Dramatic Club, and so an interest in theatre and playwriting was evident while his reputation as a prose writer was also in development.

By the late 1880s, Barrie was a published novelist, but popular acclaim arrived with the publication of *Auld Licht Idylls* in 1888, a compilation of sketches based upon his formative years and set in 'Thrums', a fictionalised version of Kirriemuir. *The Graphic* described the publication as 'a book of real humour, touching the surface of things and persons with a light and lively hand, with occasional subtle suggestions of the depths of human nature below them'.[7] This is an apt description of Barrie's work more broadly, a lightness of touch in observing and commenting upon his characters, and upon any relationship they may have to the world of his readers (or in the case of drama, audiences). Barrie did write about contemporary issues, for example about women's rights in *The Twelve Pound Look* (1910), class tension in *The Admirable Crichton* (1902), and wartime in *A Well-Remembered Voice* (1918). However, his writing is observational rather than interrogative in character, and a further early example of this is the novel *Sentimental Tommy* (1896), about an artist who navigates life through role-playing and pretence and has a devastating effect upon other people through his unwillingness to confront reality, as the sequel *Tommy and Grizel* (1900) indicates. Based in part upon his own life and failing marriage, these two prose works look inwards at the experiences of the artist, rather than outwards to the pressures creating those experiences. Similarly in his first commercial success as a playwright, the farcical comedy *Walker, London* (1892) about three couples and their progress towards marriage, R.D.S. Jack notes that Barrie is 'more concerned to amuse than instruct'.[8] Barrie does not promote a relationship between the personal and the political as a contemporary like George Bernard Shaw was doing at that time. Another characteristic of Barrie's work is how amusement is often conjoined with melancholy, for example in the play *Mary Rose* (1920), which is concerned with the inexplicable disappearance of the title character from a remote Scottish island as a child, her reappearance after a few days, and two more disappearances as a young woman. Critics have viewed this work as an attempt to show the trauma of unaccountable loss experienced by a post-war audience, but like *Peter Pan* – which of course had its origins well before the First World War – it is the tale of a child who opts out of the world rather than accepting that time's forward march and maturity are inevitable. Indeed, all of these strands to Barrie's work are evident in *Peter Pan*; it is lively, amusing, at times characterised by pathos, and presenting rather than interrogating facets of the contemporary world. These characteristic qualities conjoin with an interest in boyhood and motherhood that chimes with events and experiences in the early life of the writer.

One crucial part of Barrie's life that cannot be neglected when thinking about *Peter Pan* is the sustained relationship Barrie forged in the late 1890s with the Llewellyn Davies family. This relationship – with Barrie eventually becoming guardian to the boys after the death of their father in 1907 and then their mother in 1910 – was integral to the evolution of the play, and is the subject of much scrutiny elsewhere; for example in Birkin's intricate *J.M. Barrie and the Lost Boys: The real story behind 'Peter Pan'* (2003), and reimagined in the film *Finding Neverland* (2004). Friendship with the family resulted in regular meetings between Barrie and initially two, but eventually all five of the Llewellyn Davies boys in Kensington Gardens. It was there, at first through storytelling and play, that the character of Peter evolved. He first appeared in published form in the novel *The Little White Bird* (1902), and by December 1904, on the stage of the Duke of York's Theatre. Barrie was married to actress Mary Ansell from 1891 until they divorced in 1909, and the couple had no children which in conjunction with the intensity of his relationship with the Llewellyn Davies boys has led to suggestions of paedophilia. Prominent biographical studies of Barrie do consider this possibility and Birkin, after years of research into Barrie and the origins of the play, and after corresponding with the youngest Llewellyn Davies boy, Nico, has asserted that Barrie was 'a lover of childhood, but was not in any sexual sense the paedophile that some claim him to have been'.[9] The truth cannot now be confirmed, of course, and so the reputation of Barrie mirrors that of Lewis Carroll, as an author responsible for a defining and enduring work in the field of children's literature, who cannot now escape the shadow of suspicion linked to his fascination with children and childhood.

Barrie remained a prolific author until his death on 19th June 1937, although his new drama experienced most popularity in the first two decades of the twentieth century. Prose writing continued as well, but it is *Peter Pan* that has kept Barrie's name a familiar one for audiences of theatre and film. His status as an author was consolidated during his lifetime through honours and accolades: appointed a baronet (1913), appointed Rector of the University of St. Andrew's (1919), made a member of the Order of Merit (1922), and President of the Society of Authors (1928). Beyond his lifetime, his reputation has been bolstered by the gift of royalties from *Peter*

Pan to Great Ormond Street Hospital. This step was taken by Barrie in 1929, but Great Ormond Street Hospital Children's Charity has a right to royalty in perpetuity in the United Kingdom, an exceptional decision granted by the Copyright, Designs and Patents Act of 1988. This distinguishes the play as a unique commercial product within the mainstream entertainment industry, where it has experienced sustained prominence, nationally and internationally, since the London premiere of 1904.

Notes

1 Jacqueline Rose, *The Case of 'Peter Pan', or the Impossibility of Children's Fiction* (Philadelphia: University of Pennsylvania Press, 1992), p. xii.
2 J.M. Barrie, *Peter Pan in Peter Pan and Other Plays*, ed. by Peter Hollindale (Oxford: Oxford University Press, 1995), Act 3, p. 125. This edition of the play is used throughout unless otherwise stated.
3 Elizabeth Broadbent, 'Peter Pan and the Roots of Racism', *Huffington Post*, 11 December 2014.
4 The magical island of Never Land has been referred to in various ways since 1904, for example, Never, Never, Never Land or Neverland. For clarity within this book, Never Land is used throughout.
5 See production pages, National Theatre, www.nationaltheatre.org.uk/shows/peter-pan [accessed 16th April 2018].
6 Andrew Birkin, *J.M. Barrie and the Lost Boys*, 2nd edn (New Haven: Yale University Press, 2003), p. 5.
7 'New Novels', *The Graphic*, 12 May 1888.
8 R.D.S. Jack, 'Barrie as Journeyman-Dramatist: A Study of Walker, London', *Studies in Scottish Literature*, 22:1 (1987), pp. 60–77 (p. 62).
9 Quoted in Anthony Lane, 'Lost Boys: Why J.M. Barrie Created Peter Pan', *The New Yorker*, 22 November 2004. Hereafter in the text, Nico Llewellyn Davies is referred to as Nico Davies, the form of the name used throughout most of his life.

Chapter 1

Developing *Peter Pan* for performance

Peter Pan is frequently associated with the field of children's literature; it is often defined as a work for children and as influential upon subsequent writing aimed at young readers. However, the play was created for a cross-generational audience; four years before the play premiered, an early biography of Barrie included a chapter titled 'His Knowledge of Boys':

> It is one thing to be able to write books for boys, and another thing to be able to write books about boys. The art of pleasing the youthful reader of fiction is a comparatively easy one, but the art of entrancing adult readers with the story of a boy is given only to the few.[1]

Early reviews of *Peter Pan* also note that Barrie's depiction of childhood had appeal to an adult readership:

> The whole play must be treated as a fanciful extravaganza, written and constructed for the amusement of children, and yet there are passages in it which are worthy of Mr Barrie at his best. The piece is full of hits at

> social foibles and conventions which children will hardly appreciate, but which their elders will greatly relish.[2]

The desire to reach a cross-generational audience is certainly evident in the published play, where extensive directions signal the efforts of the playwright to create material that was immediate for an adult audience, alongside the playful content designed to engage younger viewers. For example, the characteristics to be embodied and presented by the actor playing Mr. Darling, on his first entrance:

> Mr. Darling [. . .] is really a good man as bread-winners go, and it is hard luck for him to be propelled into the room now, when if we had brought him in a few minutes earlier or later he might have made a fairer impression. In the City, where he sits on a stool all day, as fixed as a postage stamp, he is so like all the others on stools that you recognise him not by his face but by his stool, but at home the way to gratify him is to say he has a distinct personality.[3]

The reflection upon a stultifying middle-class workplace included here by Barrie could not, of course, be represented explicitly on stage, but it is evocative for an actor, and for the reader, of a particular kind of professional 'bread-winner' that would certainly be present in the 1904 audience. The implication is that the actor playing Mr. Darling should communicate, through his desire for status and respect within the household, the absence of those qualities beyond that arena. Dialogue does help to communicate this also, as in the following exchange between the character and Nana, the Newfoundland dog who is nanny to the Darling children:

> MR DARLING: Am I master in this house or is she? (*To Nana fiercely*) Come along. (*He thunders at her, but she indicates that she has reasons not worth troubling him with for remaining where she is. He resorts to a false bonhomie*) There, there, did she think he was angry with her, poor Nana? (*She wriggles a response in the affirmative*) Good Nana, pretty Nana. (*She has seldom been called pretty, and it has the old effect. She plays rub-a-dub with her paws, which is how a dog blushes*) She will come to her kind master won't she? won't she? (*She advances, retreats, waggles her head, her tail, and eventually goes to him. He seizes her collar in an iron grip and amid the cries of his progeny drags her from the room. They listen, for her remonstrances are not inaudible*)[4]

It is, of course, absurd that the animal is acting as nanny, but this section also foregrounds the absurdity of Mr. Darling's efforts at authority. Barrie wants to emphasise that Mr. Darling should evoke the idea of an inadequate and an unsatisfactory adult life; this is both comic material and evocative of anxieties around authority and status that would be familiar to significant numbers in the West End audience. The play appeals to older audiences through its confrontation of the impermanence of childhood as well as the disappointing nature of adult experience; as Carol Mavor states it is the story of 'a sweet soufflé before the time of its fall'.[5] This precise form of drama created by Barrie, communicating with a cross-generational audience but focusing upon the experiences and perspectives of children, can be more fully examined through looking at the origins of the play and the influences upon its composition.

Peter Pan in Kensington Gardens and after

'There is no definitive text of *Peter Pan* but there *is* a textual history'.[6] Here, Donna R. White and C. Anita Tarr identify the difficulty in confirming where Peter began; it is possible to expand upon their assertion to note that textual origins are not the only consideration, since the character and his imagined worlds began in the play and the storytelling undertaken by Barrie with the Llewellyn Davies boys in Kensington Gardens. An early textual version was privately printed in 1901; *The Boy Castaways of Black Lake Island* was an adventure story produced as a record of summertime games when Barrie and the Llewellyn Davies family holidayed together in Surrey. Only two copies were ever printed, but passages do parallel the story of Peter Pan that is present in the play. Then in 1902 a novel for adults, *The Little White Bird*, was published, recounting the relationship between the narrator and a couple with one young son. Within the novel, Barrie presents the story of a baby who flew out of his nursery, called Peter Pan. It is here that one characteristic feature of the stage play has its origins; aerial manoeuvres on stage developed from references to flight in this earlier prose version. Barrie uses flight in the novel to argue that the freedom found in infancy and childhood hold all the promise of a bird's flight, but are curtailed by adult expectations which manifest in, for example, the bars placed on nursery windows. This idea is retained within the published version of the play, most explicitly in the final confrontation between Peter and Hook in Act 5, Scene 1:

> HOOK 'Tis some fiend fighting me! Pan, who and what art thou?
>
> (*The children listen eagerly for the answer, none quite so eagerly as Wendy*)

PETER (*at a venture*) I'm youth, I'm joy, I'm a little bird that has broken out of the egg.

HOOK To't again!

(*He has now a damp feeling that this boy is the weapon which is to strike him from the lists of man; but the grandeur of his mind still holds and, true to the traditions of his flag, he fights on like a human flail. Peter flutters round and through and over these gyrations as if the wind of them blew him out of the danger zone, and again he darts in and jags.*)[7]

Peter Pan was staged just two years after *The Little White Bird* was published, and there is a clear relationship between prose and play. However, the play itself continued to evolve each year until Barrie's death in 1937, the author adapting and revising his text for professional presentation.

The play premiered on Broadway in 1905 and the commercial success of the London and New York productions also resulted in further prose versions of the story. In 1906, the Peter Pan chapters from *The Little White Bird* were published as *Peter Pan in Kensington Gardens*, with illustrations by Arthur Rackham. Then in 1911 came the novelisation *Peter and Wendy*; this version is very often thought to be the definitive version of the Peter Pan tale but Barrie's persistent revisions to the play text suggest that he was most committed to the story in performance.

Given these multiple early renderings of *Peter Pan*, it is worth outlining the story that is presented within the most definitive dramatic version that we have, the first published play text of 1928. Within this text, there are lengthy prose introductions to each scene accompanying stage directions and dialogue, indicating Barrie's desire to prescribe how the worlds he created within the play should be understood by readers and audiences. The opening act and much of the closing scene take place in the nursery of the Darling house in Bloomsbury, London. The three Darling children – Wendy, John, and Michael – meet Peter in this room, depart with him for Never Land, and then, at the opening of Act 5 Scene 2, are returned to their nursery. Although extensive stage directions imply that realism is present through the detail of the nursery scenes, absurd elements such as the Newfoundland dog Nana performing the actions of a nanny immediately resist straightforward dramatic realism.

A contrast between imagined ideals and material reality lies at the heart both of the play and the character of Peter, and for Barrie this was embodied through the juxtaposition of fine stage detail and fantastical action. Barrie criticised efforts to show character and environment on stage as familiar, stable entities that could adequately present the experiences of the individual. In 1891, he wrote in disapproval of drama that demonstrated this kind of effort, stating that 'to conceive of the Ibsen Drama gaining an extensive or permanent foothold on the stage is hardly possible'.[8] His response to promotion of Ibsen and his drama in the final decades of the nineteenth century had been the burlesque *Ibsen's Ghost*, produced at Toole's Theatre in London in 1891. A dramatist who could conceive of many, varied, fantastical worlds could not countenance what he perceived to be a rigid form of naturalism. Although it is hard to picture the history of European theatre without the influence of Ibsen, to Barrie, drama without the competing demands of lived experience and imagined alternatives was unsatisfactory.

Barrie does, however, insist in the opening stage directions to *Peter Pan* that precision and rigour are to be employed in depicting even the most absurd elements within his play:

> The cuckoo clock strikes six, and Nana springs into life. This first moment in the play is tremendously important, for if the actor playing Nana does not spring properly we are undone. She will probably be played by a boy, if one clever enough can be found, and must never be on two legs except on those rare occasions when an ordinary nurse would be on four. This Nana must go about all her duties in a most ordinary manner, so that you know in your bones she performs them just so every evening at six; naturalness must be her passion; indeed, it should be the aim of every one in the play, for which she is now setting the pace.[9]

Therefore, the traits of a familiar, contemporary world are usurped by intricate details that confirm, for the audience, that real and imagined worlds co-exist within his play. In the final pages of the 1928 text, the action moves away from the nursery to show that although the Darling children did return home, Wendy continues to visit Never Land; this is Barrie's appeal for us to prize imagined worlds despite our necessary existence in the real and tangible spaces we inhabit day to day beyond the theatre space.

The rest of the play is situated in Never Land, an environment that Barrie makes particular to Peter, but that is to be associated with the imaginative faculties of each individual encountering the play. This is made explicit in the published opening directions for Act 2:

> What you see is the Never Land. You have often half seen it before, or even three-quarters, after the night-lights were lit, and you might then have beached your coracle on it if you had not always at the great moment

> fallen asleep. I dare say you have chucked things on to it, the things you can't find in the morning.[10]

Events within this Never Land environment are particular 'things', dream-like set pieces that aim to prompt the imaginative faculty in spectators. While the play has a structure informed by the evolving relationship between Peter and Wendy, and the ongoing combat between Peter and Hook, each scene could be presented in isolation and would work as a set piece, and so Never Land is less an island and more an abstract environment where scenes from the imagination are made tangible. To summarise:

Act 2: Peter returns to Never Land with Wendy, who immediately takes on the role of mother to all of the lost boys. The idea of Never Land being an island of competing factions is promoted, as Hook and his crew, the pursuit of Hook by a crocodile that may be identified by the ticking of a clock it has swallowed, and a First Nations community are all introduced.

Act 3: Peter and Wendy are confronted by Hook at the Mermaids' Lagoon; Peter facilitates Wendy's escape and is prepared to drown before he is saved by sailing away in a bird's nest.

Act 4: The house under the ground inhabited by Peter, the Darling children, and the Lost Boys is shown and Wendy remains pivotal in caring for the large group of children. Above ground, the audience can see a battle between First Nations characters and Hook's band of pirates, and then as all of the children set out to leave Never Land (without Peter), they are abducted by Hook, who sneaks in to the house and attempts to poison the sleeping Peter. Tinker Bell drinks the poison to save Peter.

Act 5 Scene 1: Peter boards the pirate ship to save the children and fights Hook, who finally admits defeat and succumbs to the waiting crocodile.

The ends to Acts 3 and 4 are notable for producing the two most celebrated details of the play. It is when Peter confronts his imminent demise at the end of Act 3 that he states: 'To die will be an awfully big adventure'.[11] Then, the end of Act 4 requires the actor or actress playing Peter to engage in direct address with the audience:

> PETER [. . .] She says – she says she thinks she could get well again if children believed in fairies! (*He rises and throws out his arms he knows not to whom, perhaps to the boys and girls of whom he is not one*) Do you believe in fairies? Say quick that you believe! If you believe, clap your hands![12]

The confrontation of mortality forges some sense of connection between the scenes set in Never Land, as the revival of Tinker Bell follows the attitude to death found in the preceding scene. However, it is at the end of Act 5 Scene 1, just before all the children return to the Darling nursery, that Barrie presents the audience with what must happen between life and death: maturity. After defeating Hook, Peter is presented in a final tableau:

> *The curtain rises to show Peter a very Napoleon on his ship. It must not rise again lest we see him on the poop in Hook's hat and cigars, and with a small iron claw[.]*[13]

Therefore, after Never Land is introduced in Act 2, the rest of the time spent in that environment is used to present the audience not just with children at play, but children playing at the different stages of life they will encounter. Although *Peter Pan* is often read as Barrie's resistance to maturity and to leaving behind childhood, it operates to some extent as a meditation on the necessity of that process. This more serious consideration of progress through life is contained with dynamic family entertainment, however, and it will be helpful to consider some forms of theatre utilised by Barrie as he reworked Peter's story and his own preoccupation with mortality for the stage.

What kind of play is *Peter Pan*?

Both the 1928 play text and reviews of initial productions provide evidence of Barrie working to create theatre from the stories developed for the Llewellyn Davies boys. However, even though the play is based to some extent upon his personal experience, it is also shaped and defined by its role as a piece of seasonal entertainment. In reviewing the premiere, the critic for the *Manchester Courier and Lancashire General Advertiser* noted it was characteristic work by Barrie, stating that as a dramatist 'while he is always himself, he is never the same', and in this case the result is that 'Barrie has suddenly bethought himself that he would like to write a Christmas play' which is 'a typical production of the Barrie genius, with all the Barrie humour, the Barrie whimsicality, and the Barrie sentiment'.[14] Therefore, *Peter Pan* is both characteristic of its author and particular to the season. More specifically, *Peter Pan* as we know it is influenced by its affiliation to the British pantomime tradition.

Pantomime is now a diverse form; as Millie Taylor has identified, it falls in to four categories: Commercial, Repertory, Alternative, Amateur.[15] These different types have been propelled by developments throughout the twentieth century, including the foundation of regional repertory theatres, amateur theatre movements of the interwar years, the emergence of subsidised theatre after the Second World War, and fringe theatre work within and beyond London. Barrie's experience of pantomime as an audience member came before these developments, however, and *Peter Pan* is influenced by the form and content of professional London pantomime as it was in the final decades of the nineteenth century.

It is possible to chart the origins of this kind of pantomime performance in the mime work of Ancient Greek and Roman theatre and the Italian Renaissance *Commedia dell'arte* tradition. Characters developed within *Commedia* who worked their way into pantomime include the lovers Harlequin and Columbine, the clown Pierrot, and the skinflint Pantaloon. London theatre manager John Rich is acknowledged as importing elements of the *Commedia* tradition and establishing the Harlequinade performance in 1716 to promote his own mime and movement work in the Harlequin role; this was the earliest form of English pantomime. Initially, pantomime retold familiar stories from classical antiquity, but by the middle of the nineteenth century European fairy tale narratives were favoured, and pantomime had become a Christmas entertainment. At this stage, elements still found in pantomime today were making an appearance, particularly the characters of the Dame and the Principal Boy, roles requiring cross-gender casting.

One reason for the popularity of these cross-gender performances by the middle of the nineteenth century was the influence of burlesque – then a very popular form of theatre – upon Christmas pantomime tradition. Nineteenth-century burlesque satirised contemporary events, individuals, and pre-existing cultural products, and titles of mid-century pantomimes suggest how fairy tale and contemporary reference were being conjoined in pantomimes influenced by the burlesque tradition. For example, *Jack and the Beanstalk; or, Harlequin Leap-Year, and the Merry Pranks of the Good Little People*, performed at Drury Lane, London in 1859, makes reference to fairy tale, *Commedia*, and a contemporary pre-occupation with the coming leap year. Burlesque also often included actresses in 'breeches roles', in other words, dressed as male characters. Therefore, the Harlequin character becomes the Principal Boy character, performed by a woman in what is recognisably male attire. While pantomime has altered over time, the combination of music, movement, spectacle, and the telling of familiar tales through discrete set piece scenes has survived to this day and was evident in the pantomimes Barrie would have seen in the final decades of the nineteenth century.

This summary of pantomime tradition and history indicates the extent to which *Peter Pan* is influenced by the form. For example, the characters of Peter and Wendy echo the Harlequin (latterly Principal Boy) and Columbine (latterly Principal Girl) figures. The Harlequin character is most often conveyed as a trickster, a quality evident in the behaviour of Peter, while Columbine often out-tricks Harlequin, and this is echoed by Wendy in her ultimate command of events. For example, in the opening act of the play she gains the upper hand in negotiations with Peter, promising him more stories only if her brothers can accompany them to Never Land.

Casting a woman as Peter, usual practice until the RSC's 1982 production of the play, further emphasises the relationship to pantomime tradition. Other elements in Barrie's work that adhere to that tradition include the 'skin parts' – actors impersonating animals, playing both Nana and the crocodile that pursues Hook – and the misanthropic qualities of Hook, echoing the skinflint Pantaloon from the *Commedia* tradition and his afterlife in pantomime characters like Baron Hardup (*Cinderella*). Direct appeal to the audience – 'Do you believe in fairies?' – also reflects the influence of the popular seasonal entertainment upon evolution of the play.

Significantly, however, while *Peter Pan* was conceived as a piece for Christmas time and drew on pantomime practice, it was never categorised *as* pantomime. Early reviews recognised the parallels, the *Edinburgh Evening News* defining the play as 'a medley of farce, of fairy tale, and pantomime'.[16] However, in many ways it does not comply with pantomime convention. There is no true Dame figure, and there are scenes locating the Darling household in the recognisable, contemporary world of Edwardian London, resisting definition of the play simply as a new pantomime tale. *Peter Pan* was, rather, one example of alternatives to the pantomime found on West End stages by the beginning of the twentieth century. In 1901, Barrie took the Llewellyn Davies boys to see a new production, *Bluebell in Fairyland*:

> A very dainty and charming children's play was produced at the Vaudeville Theatre yesterday afternoon, in the shape of *Bluebell in Fairyland*, which is officially described as 'A Musical Dream Play in Two Acts.' In his libretto Mr. Seymour Hicks has dealt with an excursion of a flower girl, Bluebell, into fairyland to wake and reform

> the sleeping King, who, as a punishment for his many crimes, has been doomed to sleep away 300 years in a particularly forbidding underground cavern.[17]

As this review in the *Times* notes, the play was framed as 'Dream' rather than pantomime, and the initial description indicates that, like *Peter Pan*, the play conjoined contemporary and fairy tale worlds. *Bluebell* is one precursor to *Peter Pan*; it presented to Barrie the possibility of seasonal plays for family audiences that were not, or were not just, pantomime.

Bluebell was one inspiration alongside a number of pre-existing literary and dramatic texts that were clearly influential for the dramatist. Kirsten Stirling recognises that '[t]here *are* no Native Neverlanders – not the Redskins, not the Pirates, not even Peter Pan himself – because every detail of Neverland is, consciously or unconsciously, imported from somewhere else, and, as Barrie makes clear, in most cases from some other text'.[18] Some of these texts are quite obvious; it is hard not to perceive echoes of Robert Louis Stevenson's *Treasure Island* in the presentation of Hook's pirate entourage. Some are more abstract; in creating an island environment where magic is possible and all human residents are more or less willing immigrants, the play echoes Shakespeare's *The Tempest*.

Therefore, it is evident that *Peter Pan* was influenced by pre-existing work, included characteristic traits of Barrie's drama, and drew on pantomime tradition. This combination of influences is significant in explaining the enduring and malleable nature of the play and its appeal beyond Britain. If it were solely pantomime, it would be unlikely to resonate internationally and yet that line of influence does explain, to a significant extent, why it rapidly made its way in to the

British pantomime repertoire, a phenomenon that will be examined further in Chapter 3.

The creation of Never Land and its inhabitants

It is worth charting other, discernible influences on Barrie's theatrical imagination; a preoccupation with the ethereal and fantastic qualities of *Peter Pan* can mask the range of inspiration for this play and its stage worlds. For example, why the label Never Land for Peter's imagined realm? While no single, definite inspiration can be determined for this choice, there are uses of the term that would have been palpable for Barrie by the early 1900s. On 23rd October 1900 Israel Zangwill's one act play, *The Moment of Death; or, The Never, Never Land*, premiered in New York. The evocative title, linking mortality to an impossible world, certainly resonates with *Peter Pan*, and its author was an acquaintance of Barrie's, who sent a telegram apologising for his absence from the opening night of Zangwill's *Children of the Ghetto* in 1899.[19] Although 'Never Land' has been referred to since 1904 as Never Land, Neverland, and Never-Never Land, the earliest version for the play was 'Never, Never, Never Land' which is particularly evocative of the 1900 drama by Zangwill. The idea of a Never Land was also frequently present in the press by the final decades of the nineteenth century, as uninhabited regions in Australia were commonly referred to as 'The Never-Never'. Indeed, the term is still used, on occasion, to refer to remote outback areas of the Northern Territories and Queensland. So, for example, three months before *Peter Pan* was first staged, readers of the *Times* would find a description of 'the endless gum trees of "the bush" spreading from the coast hundreds of miles into the confines of the "Never-Never country", the Wild

West of the eastern States'.[20] While the Never Land of the play is not characterised by this sense of expanse, described in the 1928 text as a 'nicely crammed' island environment, some early reviews for the 1904 production used the format 'Never-Never', so the phrase was familiar when the play was created.[21]

Further contextual factors can be traced that surely influenced the creation of the play. Another example is the large number of character names within the play taken from acquaintances of Barrie, from works of literature he admired, and from popular history. These include the pirate character Cecco named after Cecco Hewlett, the son of Barrie's friend, novelist Maurice Hewlett, and frequent allusions to *Treasure Island* and pirate William Kidd (c. 1645–1701) in stage directions describing the pirates and their environments. A final example of direct influence upon composition of the play is that the nursery scenes described in stage directions were based directly upon the nursery in the home of renowned architect Edwin Lutyens, at 29 Bloomsbury Square. Lutyens also designed the nursery set for the 1904 production.[22] Despite his reputation as a writer concerned with childhood and imagined worlds, Barrie had one foot squarely in his day to day experience, and this informed the action and setting of the play.

The text we read, published almost a quarter of a century after the first performance, is full of details that were evidently based upon external factors, or factors that developed during performance. The next chapter examines the influence of early productions upon the play because despite the enduring fascination with personal motivations underpinning the creation of *Peter Pan*, it is essential to recognise that Barrie was a professional writer, creating work in collaboration with theatre industry professionals. Arguably, the two key influences upon the play's creation – personal incentive and production practice – resulted in a work that is both thematically complex and commercially astute, with an enduring interest for audiences.

Notes

1 J.A. Hammerton, *J.M. Barrie and His Books* (London: Horace Marshall, 1900), p. 153.
2 'Mr. Barrie's New Play', *Edinburgh Evening News*, 28 December 1904.
3 Barrie, *Peter Pan*, Act 1, p. 90.
4 Ibid., p. 96.
5 Carol Mavor, *Reading Boyishly: Roland Barthes, J.M. Barrie, Jacques Henri Lartigue, Marcel Proust, and D.W. Winnicott* (Durham, NC: Duke University Press, 2007), p. 164.
6 Donna R. White and C. Anita Tarr, 'Introduction', in *J.M. Barrie's 'Peter Pan' In and Out of Time*, ed. by Donna R. White and C. Anita Tarr (Lanham, MD: Scarecrow Press, 2006), pp. vii–xxvi (p. viii).
7 Barrie, *Peter Pan*, p. 146.
8 Writing in the *Times*, 21 April 1891; quoted in Christopher Innes, *Modern British Drama: The Twentieth Century* (Cambridge: Cambridge University Press, 2002), p. 438.
9 Barrie, *Peter Pan*, Act 1, p. 88.
10 Barrie, *Peter Pan*, Act 2, p. 105.
11 Barrie, *Peter Pan*, Act 3, p. 125.
12 Barrie, *Peter Pan*, Act 4, pp. 136–137.
13 Barrie, *Peter Pan*, Act 5, Scene 1, p. 146.
14 'Mr. Barrie's New Play: A Real Children's Pantomime', *Manchester Courier and Lancashire General Advertiser*, 28 December 1904.
15 Millie Taylor, *British Pantomime Performance* (Bristol: Intellect Books, 2007), p. 15.

16 'Mr. Barrie's New Play', *Edinburgh Evening News*, 28 December 1904.

17 'Vaudeville Theatre', *Times*, 19 December 1901.

18 Kirsten Stirling, *Peter Pan's Shadows in the Literary Imagination* (New York: Routledge, 2012), p. 21.

19 This correspondence is housed in the Zangwill Collection, Central Zionist Archives, Jerusalem, and is referenced in Meri-Jane Rochelson, 'Language, Gender, and Ethnic Anxiety in Zangwill's Children of the Ghetto', *English Literature in Transition 1880–1920*, 31:4 (1988), 399–412.

20 'Fiscal Policy and the Commonwealth', *Times*, 29 September 1904.

21 Barrie, *Peter Pan*, Act 2, p. 105; 'Our London Letter', *Aberdeen Daily Journal*, 28 December 1904; 'Peter Pan at the Duke of York's Theatre', *The Manchester Guardian*, 28 December 1904.

22 Correspondence relating to this detail is held in the Production File for *Peter Pan*, Duke of York's Theatre, 1904, V&A Theatre & Performance Department.

Chapter 2

First performances

The spectacle and narrative of the play are underpinned by an interrogation of how and why we continue to find the experiences and perspectives of childhood desirable, an interrogation embodied in the ethereal character of Peter. Jacqueline Rose argues that this tension sustains the appeal:

> The material investment in 'Peter Pan' has been vast, matched only by a seemingly contradictory investment in Peter Pan as an ethereal substance, or disembodied child, unstained by lucre or blood. In the case of 'Peter Pan', the two conceptions – of money and innocence – appear to go hand in hand, endlessly calling each other up and cancelling each other out.[1]

This tension between commercially viable and thematically sophisticated elements was consolidated through the first production of *Peter Pan*, which opened at the Duke of York's Theatre on 27th December 1904. The play was originally supposed to open on 22nd December but one day earlier a mechanical lift being used on stage collapsed, destroying a great deal of the scenery, forcing the delay. From the beginning, a piece ostensibly concerned with escape to the ethereal realm of Never Land has been overshadowed by the material concerns of the theatre space. This is a technically demanding play, requiring set, lighting, and machinery for stage flight, as well as the co-ordination of a large cast, made up at least in part of child actors.

The 1904 production process

The first production had to be supported by a commercial theatre maker who was sympathetic towards these requirements. Andrew Birkin notes the reaction of one potential producer to the play, London actor-manager Herbert Beerbohm Tree, when Barrie read the script to him in March 1904. Tree immediately wrote a response to producer Charles Frohman:

> Barrie has gone out of his mind [. . .] I'm sorry to say it, but you ought to know it. He's just read me his new play. He is going to read it to you, so I'm warning you. I know I have not gone woozy in my mind, because I have tested myself since hearing the play, but Barrie must be mad.[2]

Frohman did not heed the warning, however, as he was the first producer for *Peter Pan*, in London and then New York. Indeed, what almost certainly prompted Tree to write to the American producer was the knowledge that Frohman very often produced Barrie's work; for example, Frohman had already produced both *Quality Street* and *The Admirable Crichton* in London in 1902.

Barrie first met Frohman when he travelled to New York in 1896, and the men became friends as well as business partners. Frohman's biographers note the importance of close friendship to the work of the producer, friendship 'often made in the theatrical world of make-believe, but always cemented in the domain of very sincere reality'.[3] This is not unusual within the theatre industry, where creative collaboration can benefit from sustained personal relationships, but it is striking that both 'make-believe' (imagination) and 'reality' (professional practice) are recognised as valuable to Frohman in his work, factors which may explain an enduring working relationship between the two men. Certainly, despite the consistent drive for profit evident in the career of Frohman, his personal, passionate commitment to *Peter Pan* was clear. A casualty, in 1915, of the sinking by a German U-boat of the trans-Atlantic ocean liner the Lusitania, Frohman is reported to have paraphrased the best-known line from *Peter Pan* when death was imminent with the words: 'Why fear death? It is the most beautiful adventure that life gives us'.[4]

In his working life, Frohman operated along similar lines to the major producers that still dominate West End and Broadway production, controlling multiple venues and mounting a number of productions concurrently. After spending some years working in box office, stage management, and as a touring manager, Frohman set up as an independent New York producer in 1885, embodying the emerging professional-managerial class in commercial theatre. For example, he centralised the booking process for many out-of-town venues, providing a service that was separate, but supplementary, to New York productions. This demonstrated a concerted effort to offset the risk of theatrical production and to work on a national, not just a local, level. In 1896, he was one of six leading New York producers and booking agents to form the Theatrical Syndicate, ensuring a monopoly of mainstream theatre production on tour and in key cities nationwide.[5]

During the 1890s, work in London commenced with comedy *This Happy Life* by Louis N. Parker presented at the Duke of York's Theatre in December 1897. Frohman leased a number of West End venues including the Duke of York's, where he had staged *Crichton*, Barrie's most successful play to date. Since 1901, the producer had employed Dion Boucicault to co-ordinate productions at the venue, and in the programme for *Peter Pan* it is noted that the play is 'under the Direction of' Boucicault. Although during the first decade of the twentieth century we are still some way from the figure of the theatre director as it is conceived today, it is possible to label Boucicault as director of *Peter Pan* in 1904, since he supervised the translation of Barrie's initial script to the stage. He was the eldest surviving son of the renowned nineteenth-century playwright Dion Boucicault and, after working as an actor and theatre manager in London, New York, and Australia (on tour, then in both Melbourne and Sydney), he took up work for Frohman at the Duke of York's.

In an era when many London venues were still run by actor-managers – theatre entrepreneurs like Tree who either owned or leased a theatre, managed the site, and most often starred within the productions mounted there – the practice at the Duke of York's theatre of employing a director figure shows Frohman operating differently. As a trans-Atlantic entrepreneur, he aimed to stage a number of productions at the same time, in more than one country, and needed on-site representatives to enable that process. The managerial and creative structures put in place by Frohman resemble West End theatre making as it was to develop in the twentieth century. Therefore the first production of *Peter Pan* was characterised by progressive commercial production practice, with a key creative trio – Barrie, Boucicault, and Frohman – responsible for the production.

Before directing Barrie's play, Boucicault had some knowledge of and sympathy with the work of the playwright. He had previously worked on Barrie's *The Wedding Guest* (1900), *A Platonic Friendship* (1901), and then *Crichton*, but there was also a personal connection. His wife, Irene Vanbrugh, was an actress favoured by Barrie; she was a frequent collaborator with the playwright and the first person to present many of his best-known female characters on stage. The first role over which she had this measure of control was Thea Tesman in the burlesque *Ibsen's Ghost* (1891). She also played the major role of Lady Mary Lasenby in *Crichton*. Five decades after initial success in Barrie's burlesque, she still looked to her friendship with him to help frame her autobiography *To Tell My Story* (1948), reproducing correspondence from Barrie that includes reference to his characteristic preoccupation with real and imagined worlds:

> I suggest a quiet chapter somewhere about what you think of it all – the world you love when playing a part and the world outside it in which you are a different person. How to break out of the one into the other, and which of those two you are when you are truly awake.[6]

While Vanbrugh was not cast in *Peter Pan*, it is worth noting her close working relationship and enduring friendship with Barrie from the 1890s onwards; the dramatist was creating material for a familiar network of West End theatre professionals. *Peter Pan* was translated to the stage by Boucicault, linked to the playwright not only through previous collaborations but through a sustained friendship intensified by the closeness of Barrie and Vanbrugh. As with Frohman, there is evidence of sympathy for Barrie and his work that Boucicault as director could bring to the 1904 production.

Casting and character

While theatre making is often characterised by collaboration prompted by both professional and personal points of connection, this was really acute with the first London production of *Peter Pan*.[7] In addition to pre-existing relationships within the production team, the first actress to play the title role was Boucicault's sister, Nina. Hook was first embodied by an uncle of the Llewellyn Davies boys, Gerald du Maurier, who was a sibling of their mother Sylvia. Although neither Nina Boucicault nor du Maurier had been first choice for those roles, their eventual casting extended the personnel working on the production who were already closely acquainted with Barrie and his work.[8]

In casting *Peter Pan*, the decision had been made to use an adult for Peter. Frohman was particularly influential in having an adult actress in the role, foreseeing difficulties in employing a child for this leading character, and in turn having to cast all the child characters according to their ages within the text. However, there is some correspondence between Barrie and the first actress to play Peter in New York, Maude Adams, that indicates his enthusiasm for a woman in the title role:

> My Dear Maudie,
> I have written a play for children, which I don't suppose would be much use in America. She is rather a dear of a girl with ever so many children long before her hair is up and the boy is Peter Pan in a new world.

> I should like you to be the boy and the girl and most of the children and the pirate captain. I hope you are coming here before summer is ended and I also hope I may have something to read you and tell you about.[9]

Although Barrie is playful over the role Adams might take on, this letter confirms that both he and Frohman had decided upon an adult to play Peter, and the rest of the play was then cast according to the suitability of other adult actors for the roles they had to embody; a kind of 'age-blind' casting was initiated. In later correspondence about the first production, Nico Davies suggested that Barrie had quite definite ideas about age and character:

> From what he told me – and it was frequently pretty difficult, if not impossible, to know what he really meant – it was highly desirable if not, indeed, essential that the man to play Captain Hook should also be Mr. Darling. Ideally, he would say, Mrs. Darling should be played by someone impossibly young to have children as old as John and Wendy and Mr. Darling should really not be all that much older.[10]

The implication is that these youthful adults should have lost full access to the child's perspective in the play, but should still have some evident, preferably visible connection to that perspective. Even without casting 'impossibly young' parents this element survives, for example in Mr. Darling's reluctance to take his medicine in Act 1.

However, the casting of adults for most of the major roles including Peter and Wendy did alter how the play was understood in performance. In 1904 Nina Boucicault was the oldest of the principal performers in the cast at 37, du Maurier was 31, Dorothea Baird, as Mrs. Darling, was 29, and Hilda Trevelyan, as Wendy, was 24. Within the Darling family only the brothers were played by child actors; George Hersee as John – listed as 'Master' George Hersee in the programme, confirming youthful status – and Winifred Geoghegan as Michael. The practice of casting most of the key roles in stage productions of *Peter Pan* according to the expertise and renown of performers, with age as a less immediate concern, was initiated by this first production. Arguably, this encourages audiences to perceive the stage world as a fantasy realm in Act 1 well before the journey to Never Land. If audiences for the 1904 production thought about age at all, it would be to confront the fact that it had no currency or relevance to the characters depicted, and this was not a play to be judged by the standards of theatrical realism.

Casting of this production was clearly influenced by the qualities already noted: expertise and renown. For example in the year before taking on the role of Peter, Nina Boucicault had appeared in the Barrie comedy *Little Mary*.[11] Beyond her work in his drama, Boucicault was also an experienced and established West End actress; a notable period at an earlier stage of her career was two years in the first production of *Charley's Aunt* from 1892. This level of experience was valuable for a production like *Peter Pan* that required physical dexterity as well as emotional range. Boucicault was acknowledged by many reviewers to have brought complexity and poignancy to the character of Peter, the *Times* reviewer for example noting that 'Miss Nina Boucicault, as Peter Pan, knows well how to blend pathos and frolicsomeness'.[12]

The depiction of Peter was in part an experienced actress responding to the text, but evidence suggests it was also a response to the abstract nature of Peter – not quite human, but a runaway child and so not quite of Never Land – that was never clarified for Nina Boucicault in rehearsal:

> When I first began to study the part of Peter Pan, I remember going to Sir James Barrie and asking him, since I was to be the first Peter, if he would tell me something of his conception of the part and how it should be played. I thought that he would naturally have a great deal to say on the subject, that he might perhaps explain to me how he visualized Peter, and give me his ideas as to how the character should be developed. But I was doomed to disappointment. 'Peter is a bird,' he said to me in that quiet, level voice of his, 'and he is one day old.' And that is all I had to go on.[13]

Andrew Birkin notes that Boucicault was so relieved at a positive response from the first audience, she began to cry.[14] While this actress had the expertise required for the role, the challenge of the task is evident. The first night reaction shows relief at an enthusiastic reception after a difficult rehearsal process and a delayed opening night: this is a reminder that, while *Peter Pan* is deemed a magical story, the text we read today and the iconic status of the play are intrinsically linked to the work of particular performers in the first years of production for this technically demanding drama.

Looking at precise details from the first production, we see further examples of the play as we know it now developing through initial performances. Publicity photographs confirm that in the treetop scene of Act II, Peter and Wendy are connected through an embrace (see Figure 2.1):

Figure 2.1 'Miss Nina Boucicault & Miss Hilda Trevelyan' (1904), seated in a little house with Trevelyan-Wendy [R] placing her arm around Boucicault-Peter [L].

However, the 1928 text insists that '*[h]e is never touched by any one in the play*'.[15] The implication is that the character and the function of Peter were explored extensively in performance, before the author created the textual version of the drama available to us today. Early stage versions were an opportunity to hone the more complex and abstract elements of the play, as the stage set for Never Land, and performance, allowed for exploration of character.

There is evidence that Barrie built quite consciously upon this first production to develop *Peter Pan*. In a document written to assist with preparations for the American premiere in 1905, 'On the Acting of a Fairy Play', Barrie provides guidance to the company, based upon experience of the 1904 production:

> In a fairy play you may have many things to do that are not possible in real life, but you conceive yourself in a world in which they are ordinary occurrences, and act accordingly. Never do anything because there is an audience, but only and entirely because you think this is how the character in the fanciful world would do it.[16]

There is an essential need to communicate with the audience, of course; so in translating the fairy play into performance, elements including costume and stage effect worked to unite the material and the 'fanciful'. In early stage versions Tinker Bell was not represented by an actress wearing wings and gauze, but through coloured light conveying character and purpose. Boucicault's costume was of fabric fastened with laces which created an impression of Peter being covered in deteriorating vegetation, enlivened with feathers and flowers, merging the character with the Never Land environment. Both of these examples demonstrate how costuming and stage technology were used to evoke a world beyond 'real life' to support a cast in their presentation of Barrie's fantasy. Barrie also knew the importance of collaboration with performers to develop his texts and showed a sustained interest in embodied meaning within and beyond the theatre. This is demonstrated in a letter to the actress Stella Patrick Campbell in November 1921:

> I find the person who writes with his left is quite another pair of shoes from the one who employs his right; he has other standards, sleeps differently, has novel views on the ontology of being, and is a more sinister character.[17]

The 1904 production of *Peter Pan* featured for the first time that most celebrated left-hander, Captain Hook. This was a character who most certainly evolved through the work of the first actor to play the part. Gerald du Maurier created an iconic pirate figure who merged with a precise form of English upper-class sensibility. Educated at Harrow, du Maurier made his stage debut in 1894 and worked consistently in West End theatre and regularly in Barrie's drama, appearing in *Crichton* and also *Little Mary* in the two years before his appearance as both Mr. Darling and Hook. French actor Sacha Guitry praised the way du Maurier used his personality within his acting: 'To be able to project and impose his unusual personality, his intelligence, his wit and his charm, as he does, is the mark of a truly great actor'.[18] Certainly, while multiple aspects of early stage productions made their way in to the 1928 published text, du Maurier's gentleman pirate is firmly embedded there, and the association between actor and role was endorsed by du Maurier himself who stated that Hook 'was the only part I ever really liked playing'.[19]

As Daphne du Maurier noted of her father's performance, 'Gerald *was* Hook'.[20] Describing his presentation of the role, she argues that instilling fear in the audience through this character was a definite aim of the first production:

> How he was hated, with his flourish, his poses, his dreaded diabolical smile! That ashen face, those blood-red lips, the long, dank, greasy curls; the sardonic laugh, the maniacal scream, the appalling courtesy of his gestures; and that above all most terrible of moments when he descended the stairs and with slow, most merciless cunning poured the poison into Peter's glass.[21]

Significantly, Daphne du Maurier notes, her father's Hook presented, for the audience, 'Father-but-for-the-grace-of-God'; by implication the rather ineffectual Mr. Darling would be a relief, in comparison, at the end of the play.[22] The actor playing Hook (and usually Mr. Darling) is the most prominent representative of the adult on stage in this play, and du Maurier's performance was integral to making *Peter Pan* engaging for cross-generational audiences. That performance was called 'lurid' by the *Times* reviewer and 'charming' in the *Illustrated London News*, suggesting the tension between pantomime villain and English gentleman that characterised the presentation.[23] Subsequently, du Maurier's Hook becomes the Hook of the published text, employing public school jargon and insisting upon his credentials as a gentleman. Responding to the work of du Maurier, the text asks that the actor portraying Hook depicts an Englishman who channels particular class, as well as character associations, murmuring 'Floreat Etona' as he goes to his death, and in costume mimicking 'the dandiacal associated with Charles II [. . .]'.[24]

Patrick B. Tuite suggests that du Maurier presented 'a tragic and sinister royalist living in painful exile' and, certainly, his was a pirate drawn from the English aristocracy.[25] The actor played Hook for three seasons, from 1904 until 1906, and then came back to the roles of Mr. Darling and Hook in 1929. Nico Davies describes the influence of du Maurier upon the version of Hook found in the play text:

> Do you remember in the underground scene in *Peter Pan* all the children down below waiting to fly home when they hear the noise of the battle up above them between the redskins and the pirates, and the redskins are defeated and the pirates beat the tom-tom, and the boys go up the trunk of the tree to be tossed like bales of hay by the victorious pirates? However, when it's Wendy's turn to go up the tree trunk and one of the pirates is about to seize her and toss her away, Captain Hook goes to this pirate, hooks him away and in the most perfect gentlemanly fashion offers his arm to Wendy and escorts her offstage. Barrie always said that this was the test of a Captain Hook, how he offered his arm to Wendy, and without any shadow of doubt the best arm offered her was Gerald du Maurier's.[26]

Davies implies here that this standard practice for Hook was generated and defined in work undertaken by *both* Barrie and du Maurier, reiterating the role of early cast members in defining key physical action and characterisation that is now embedded in the play text.

'No one is going to catch me, lady, and make me a man': *Peter Pan* in revival[27]

To emphasise Peter's perpetual state of childhood, Barrie provided the subtitle for his play *The Boy Who Would Not Grow Up*. In practice, the immense popularity and therefore commercial viability of the play on both sides of the Atlantic served to reiterate this aspect of the character. While Barrie continued to rework the text, each year the same essential story returned to the stage and whether the same actress portrayed Peter over many years or only appeared in one production, returning audiences would see the same story of perpetual youth housed within changing theatre productions. By 1964, the diamond jubilee for the play in production, it was estimated that thirty-six million people worldwide were watching a version of *Peter Pan* each year, and it had by that time been translated into fourteen languages.[28]

The first London production was followed by a New York premiere. After a short trial at the National Theater in Washington, it opened on 6th November 1905 at the Empire Theater in New York, running until 9th June 1906 before it went on tour featuring Maude Adams, the star of the Empire production, as Peter. Adams had an established career when she took on the role, having worked in Frohman productions since 1890, and in plays by Barrie including *The Little Minister* (1897) and *Quality Street* (1901). Playwright and actress met for the first time in 1896, and had a sustained professional relationship as exemplified in their correspondence about *Peter Pan*.

Early reviews imply that Adams presented both the physical dexterity and the intermittent sorrow of the character, foregrounding multiple characteristics of Peter, for example:

> Maude Adams is Peter – most ingratiatingly simple and sympathetic. True to the fairy idea, true to the child nature, lovely, sweet, and wholesome. She combines all the delicate sprightliness and the gentle, wistful pathos necessary to the role, and she is supremely in touch with the spirit of it all.[29]

The reference to pathos echoes reviews of Boucicault in the role, but to a greater extent than was the case for that first Peter, Adams' career came to be defined by the part; she was the only actress to play the role in the United States between 1905 and 1916.

Returning to the London stage, *Peter Pan* became an annual production after the 1904 premiere, and national tours were mounted also, but Boucicault did not reprise the role. For, in December 1905, the actress Cecilia (Cissie) Loftus took on the part in London and presented the title character as less melancholy and more vital than the 1904 iteration. Loftus began working in the theatre in 1893, and her technique as an actress was influenced by experience of appearing in music and variety halls as a 'caricaturist', doing impressions of well-known performers including Dan Leno, Sarah Bernhardt, and Marie Lloyd. This kind of performance work provided experience of interaction with the audience that could feed in to *Peter Pan*. Interviewed in the first year of her career, Loftus noted, 'I like the familiarity of the audience, because I think it is a sign of affection, and every artist covets public liking. Applause from the stalls is very pleasant, but nothing is more gratifying than the working man's "Good old Cissie!" from the gallery'.[30] What this actress brought to the role was confidence with audience interaction, vital for the appeal to the audience to perform their belief in fairies and clap to save Tinker Bell at the end of Act 4. Loftus also employed a sprightly demeanour, presenting an 'elfin' character at home in the Never Land environment.[31]

Loftus, like Boucicault, only appeared for one season as Peter, and in 1906, American-born actress Pauline Chase, who had played the First Twin in earlier London productions of the play, was promoted to the title role. Chase then appeared for eight seasons, each year until 1913. Other actresses, most notably Zena Dare, were appearing as Peter for British tours, but Chase at the Duke of York's was intrinsically linked to the burgeoning Peter Pan 'industry', the publications and merchandise emerging around the annual London production. For example, in 1909 the published book *Peter Pan's Postbag*, a selection of correspondence to the actress from fans of her work in the role, was sold in the foyer of the Duke of York's Theatre. The enduring association of Chase with Peter is demonstrated by the fact that almost four decades after last playing the part, the actress was mentioned in a House of Commons debate as an American whose defining work in the role is used, here, to make a point about employment law:

> In the Commons, Tory M.P. Mr. C. Fletcher-Cooke brought up the name of Pauline Chase [. . .] by agreeing with the Barrie judgement of her.
>
> 'The greatest Peter Pan in history,' said Mr. Fletcher-Cooke, in an interlude on labour permits – 'and she was an American.'[32]

Boucicault had been defined, in critical responses, as an ethereal Peter foregrounding pathos; Loftus as a physical, vital character. Chase arguably combined these traits, presenting both energy and fragility so that the *Daily Chronicle* reviewer remarked 'Miss Chase brings Peter Pan nearer to being a boy fairy than any of her predecessors'.[33] The actress could of course develop a character based upon both her own technical abilities and upon her observation of both Boucicault and Loftus in the role. The result was an energetic, physical character who could also represent the darker content of the play: Peter as impossible, perpetual youth:

> Her Peter is something less eerie, less a being of another world than Miss Loftus made him, more of the essential human boy. The peculiar individual pathetic charm which Miss Boucicault gave to the character is changed to something which is more like the pathos of the very idea of childhood.[34]

Like Adams in America, Chase became a defining Peter through the combination of humanity and affliction brought to the role and through long association with the part.

Other actors and actresses had lengthy associations with early productions of *Peter Pan*, and so had an influence in shaping the text we read today. For example, the work of Chase as Peter took place over eight years, but this is a modest commitment to one role in the play compared to George Shelton as the pirate Smee; he appeared in the London production every year from 1904 until 1929. Hilda Trevelyan, through her repeated appearances in the play for seven London productions between 1904 and 1914, was essential to the version of Wendy Darling found in the play today, and the rest of her career was frequently defined in relation to that role. For example, going in to management at the Vaudeville Theatre in London in 1912, *The Sketch* reported her new enterprise under the headline 'At the House near Strand's Top: Manager Wendy'.[35]

Working with the play regularly over a number of years, these performers observed and participated in the evolution of both the text and its reputation. It was Trevelyan who, in the 1930s, suggested that this early period of development had turned in to something else, that annual revivals had become less dynamic, and more an act of veneration. In an obituary for Trevelyan published November 1959, Eric Johns highlighted her opinion on the annual London revival of *Peter Pan*:

> Though enormously proud of having created Wendy, and at the same time eager to preserve the Barrie tradition, Miss Trevelyan maintained, even more than 20 years ago, that *Peter Pan* ought to be given an entirely new production. She considered the annual revival seen in London to be no more than a poor carbon copy of the original production of 1904. In her opinion it needed to be staged as if it were a new play.[36]

Trevelyan's concerns are perhaps understandable as an annual London production continued uninterrupted from 1904 until 1939. Now, however, *Peter Pan* is not associated with this kind of regular revival; as detailed in the final chapter, since the mid-twentieth century, the play has most often been seen 'as if [. . .] new', through adaptation.

Notes

1 Jacqueline Rose, *The Case of 'Peter Pan'*, p. 88.
2 J.M. Barrie, *Peter Pan, or, the Boy Who Would Not Grow Up*, introduction by Andrew Birkin (London: The Folio Society, 1992), p. xxv.
3 Isaac F. Marcosson and Daniel Frohman, *Charles Frohman: Manager and Man* (London: John Lane, 1916), p. 253.
4 These words were attributed to Frohman within the weeks following the sinking of the Lusitania, as numerous articles on eminent passengers who lost their lives appeared within the North American press. See for example '"Why fear death?" Say Heroes of the Sea', *The Ogden Standard*, 19 June 1915.
5 For further information on the Syndicate and the rise of the modern producer figure in North America, see Michael Schwartz, *Broadway and Corporate Capitalism: The Rise of the Professional-Managerial Class, 1900–1920* (New York: Palgrave Macmillan, 2009).
6 Barrie's correspondence, quoted in Irene Vanbrugh, *To Tell My Story* (London: Hutchinson, 1948), p. 28.
7 For more on interpersonal relationships and theatre making, see the study by Michael R. Olssen, 'All the World's a Stage: The Information Practices and Sense-Making of Theatre Professionals', *Libri*, 60 (2010), 241–252.
8 Maude Adams, who was to play Peter in New York, in 1905, was considered for this London production but commitment to a New York production of Barrie's *The Little Minister* prevented her being cast. Seymour Hicks was first choice for Hook and Mr. Darling, with his wife, Ellaline Terriss, to play Wendy. However, when Terriss was unavailable the arrangement fell through and du Maurier was cast.
9 Correspondence from Barrie to Adams, 18 April 1904, quoted in Bruce K. Hanson, *Peter Pan on Stage and Screen 1904–2010*, 2nd edn (Jefferson, NC: McFarland & Company, 2011), p. 52.
10 Letter from Nico Davies to Christopher Calthrop, 15 December 1964, held in Production File for *Peter Pan*, Duke of York's Theatre, 1904, V&A Theatre & Performance Department. It

is difficult to determine the extent to which Barrie wrote for specific actors; just eight days earlier on 7th December, Calthrop received a letter from Roger Lancelyn Green stating: 'Barrie certainly intended that a separate actor should play Mr. Darling, and had to cut his lines at the end of the first act when Du Maurier doubled it with Hook – as he would have had no time to change'. (This correspondence also held in this Production File). However, Barrie's sustained working relationships and friendships with specific theatre professionals and, in the case of Boucicault and du Maurier their extended family, do appear to be more than coincidence with the development of *Peter Pan*.

11 This play ran at Wyndham's Theatre, produced by Frohman, from 24 September 1903 until 25 March 1904.

12 'Duke of York's Theatre', *Times*, 28 December 1904.

13 Nina Boucicault interviewed in 1923, quoted in Hanson, *Peter Pan on Stage and Screen*, p. 29.

14 Andrew Birkin, *J.M. Barrie and the Lost Boys*, p. 117.

15 Barrie, *Peter Pan*, Act 1, p. 98.

16 Roger Lancelyn Green, *Fifty Years of 'Peter Pan'* (London: Peter Davies, 1954), p. 105.

17 Viola Meynell, ed., *Letters of J.M. Barrie* (London: Peter Davies, 1942), pp. 38–39.

18 Quoted in the *Sunday Times*, 1955, precise date not found, cutting in the Biographical File for Gerald du Maurier, V&A Theatre & Performance Department.

19 'Entr'Actes No. 27; Gerald du Maurier', *Daily Sketch*, 2 December 1932.

20 Daphne du Maurier, *Gerald: A Portrait* (London: Gollancz, 1934), p. 110.

21 Ibid.

22 Ibid., p. 111.

23 'Duke of York's Theatre', *Times*, 28 December 1904; 'The Playhouses', *Illustrated London News*, 7 January 1905.

24 Barrie, *Peter Pan*, Act 5, Scene 1, p. 146; Act 2, p. 108.

25 Patrick B. Tuite, '"Shadow of [a] Girl", An Examination of Peter Pan in Performance', in *Second Star to the Right: Peter Pan in the Popular Imagination*, ed. by Allison B. Kavey and Lester D. Friedman (New Brunswick: Rutgers University Press, 2009), pp. 105–131 (p. 110).
26 Quoted in Sheridan Morley, 'Daphne du Maurier Evokes Her Father, Sir Gerald, the Last of the Great Edwardian Actor-Managers', *The Listener*, 9 August 1973.
27 Barrie, *Peter Pan*, Act 5, Scene 2, p. 151.
28 These figures come from an article celebrating the diamond jubilee for the play in production: 'The Story Behind the Story of Peter Pan', *Daily Mail*, 17 December 1964.
29 'A Joyous Night with Peter Pan', *New York Times*, 7 November 1905.
30 'The Art of the Player', *The New Weekly*, n.d., cutting in the Biographical File for Cissie Loftus, V&A Theatre & Performance Department.
31 Green, *Fifty Years of 'Peter Pan'*, p. 123.
32 Shirley Lowe, 'Peter Pan Still Refuses to Grow Up', *Daily Express*, 12 December 1953.
33 The *Daily Chronicle* review is quoted in Hanson, *Peter Pan on Stage and Screen*, p. 91.
34 'Peter Pan: The Third Year', *The Telegraph*, 19 December 1906.
35 'At the House Near Strand's Top: Manager Wendy', *The Sketch*, 4 September 1912.
36 Newspaper unknown, obituary published 12 November 1959, held in the Biographical File for Hilda Trevelyan, V&A Theatre & Performance Department.

Chapter 3

Adapting *Peter Pan*

Writing in 2004, one hundred years after the play premiered, Peter Hollindale noted that 'Barrie's text has lent itself to revision and adaptation from the start, with the author's blessing; he himself was a compulsive reviser'.[1] While it is certainly true that Barrie reworked the play text throughout his lifetime, the story continued to be seen almost exclusively in stage productions prioritising that text. It was not until the second half of the twentieth century that translation of the source play in to different forms including pantomime, musical theatre, and film began to occur regularly. Adaptations to film in particular have influenced ideas of the narrative and characters we associate with the title *Peter Pan*. It is circulation through frequent adaptation that has created what Sarah Cardwell refers to as a 'meta-text'; *Peter Pan* has become 'a valuable story or myth that is constantly growing and developing, being retold, reinterpreted and reassessed', so pervasive that we now find elements first seen in the play in innumerable texts and performances more or less identifiable as versions of that play.[2] This chapter assesses how far the story has travelled from its appearance on the West End stage in 1904.

Stage adaptations

The emergence of *Peter Pan* in adaptation was prompted in part by the annual London stage production in the first half of the twentieth century. As noted in the previous chapter, this regular revival did suggest the perpetual youth and enduring presence of Peter and Never Land, but simultaneously conveyed a sense of stasis. For example, the actress Jean Forbes-Robertson played the role nine times between 1927 and 1938, following Adams and Chase in forging a long association with the part.

The Forbes-Robertson productions were not without innovation; indeed the actress influenced the published text of the play, encouraging Barrie to foreground the physical and emotional distance between Peter and other characters:

PETER You mustn't touch me.
WENDY Why?
PETER No one must ever touch me.
WENDY Why?
PETER I don't know.[3]

It is apparent that her work in the role was characterised by a sense of Peter as poised between human and supernatural worlds, the *Times* reviewer noting that Forbes-Robertson's Peter was one 'who hovers most brilliantly between the joy and melancholy of boyhood, and the different joy and melancholy of the immortals'.[4] The work of Forbes-Robertson in the role for consecutive London seasons (from 1927 until 1934, before returning to the part once more in 1938) consolidated certain character traits now evident in the play text. Alongside this influence, the repeated presence of one actress in the role demonstrated a *habit* of *Peter Pan* on stage that had developed in London, the very thing that had troubled Hilda Trevelyan.

The publication of the play text in 1928 only exacerbated this sense of habitual practice. So, for example, when Eva Le Gallienne mounted a production of *Peter Pan* at her Civic Repertory Theatre in New York in that same year, she retained most of the narrative and language as set out in the newly published text. While the production involved some innovation, for example Le Gallienne extending the flight sequences out in to the auditorium, this was explicitly Barrie's play. Both the text and the history of the play on stage dominated theatrical presentations, and this continued beyond Barrie's lifetime. Two decades later, in post-war London, productions were still compared to early stage versions:

> Miss Margaret Lockwood does not get out of the part what some actresses have got out of it (perhaps after planting it there first) but she strikes us as being the kind of Peter with whom, when we were eight or nine and really sophisticated, we should instantly have fallen in love; so we may say Miss Lockwood does very well.[5]

As this *Times* reviewer implies, noted actresses of the time such as Lockwood, who first played Peter in 1949, found their stage authority, and indeed celebrity, subsumed within not only the character of Peter, but also the history of the play in production. If, as Michael Quinn has suggested, celebrity usually infiltrates a performance and so 'personal qualities of the individual actor dominate the perception of the actor's references to the fictional events', these annual revivals of *Peter Pan* resisted such a process. A history of Peters, rather than the status and the performance of an actress taking on the role, was dominant for returning audiences.[6] When prominent celebrities like Lockwood could not escape the history of *Peter Pan* as a defining point of reference for their own London performance, the play had become essentially tied to its origins on the West End stage at the turn of the century.

The history of adapting *Peter Pan* is a history of consciously manipulating performance type to displace the early stage history and re-present Peter in a different time, in a different cultural context, or with a different aesthetic, capitalising upon emerging performance technologies – like computer-generated imagery (CGI) in film – and offering an alternative to the initial stage model. Most often, precise conditions of copyright law over time have been cited as determining which versions of *Peter Pan* could emerge. However, it is not only legislation, but a changing entertainment industry that has become influential. By adapting the play, practitioners sought to escape comparisons to Edwardian staging practices, while benefitting from what Margherita Laera has referred to as 'the attractive familiarity' of a renowned source.[7]

On stage, the most conspicuous early examples of such adaptation were the two American musicals of 1950 and 1954. More specifically, the 1950 production was initially planned as a musical adaptation, but ultimately remained a prose version, with original accompanying music composed by Leonard Bernstein. In July 1954, the musical *Peter Pan* starring Mary Martin opened in San Francisco, with a Broadway transfer and premiere on 20th October. Martin was a prominent star of musical theatre, the first actress to play Nellie Forbush in *South Pacific* (1949) and Maria von Trapp in *The Sound of Music* (1959). She collaborated with a team including director Jerome Robbins and lyricist Carolyn Leigh to develop

Peter Pan in to what we would now define as a Golden Age Broadway musical. This was an explicit translation of the source play, the musical form radically altering the presentation of Peter. *New York Times* critic Brooks Atkinson wrote: 'Peter Pan may have been a proper Victorian originally. He is a healthy fun-loving American boy now'.[8] Although the *Peter Pan* of 1904 had been a trans-Atlantic project, co-ordinated by Frohman, here the staunchly American adaptation created a new product, allowing for different versions of character and different priorities to emerge from within the narrative. For example, the musical revises the conclusion to show Peter returning to take Wendy's daughter with him to Never Land, a strategy that could indefinitely defer implications of mortality, producing the positive ending expected of a Golden Age musical.[9]

The first production ran on Broadway until 26th February 1955. It was then transmitted in a live television broadcast by NBC on 7th March. This began regular broadcasts of the *Peter Pan* musical starring Martin over almost two decades. These had ceased by 1973 but a recording was shown once more in 1989, and then in 2014 NBC revisited the practice, broadcasting *Peter Pan Live!* which was the same musical, now starring Alison Williams as Peter and Christopher Walken as Hook. The emergence of the mid-century Broadway musical and associated live broadcasts portrayed how rapidly new traditions of performing the story became established; certainly the 2014 *Live!* broadcast situates the musical and its source play as a traditional, seasonal output for NBC. This was a strategic move by the broadcaster, nostalgically recalling the rise of network television in an era when competition from digital platforms such as Netflix was becoming a concern. In relation to *Peter Pan*, the production acts as a reminder that for

North American audiences the 1954 musical, disseminated widely through television broadcast, *is* the traditional version.

This musical adaptation was exported to Britain in 1985, with Bonnie Langford taking on the leading role. However, the most frequent stage adaptations of *Peter Pan* seen in Britain in recent decades are pantomimes. The relationship between the source play and pantomime made this an understandable development; indeed there is some evidence that the regular, seasonal, London productions had been closely associated with the pantomime form. In his review of *Peter Pan* at the RSC in 1982, Michael Billington recollected London productions of the play by the mid-twentieth century as 'that simplified and often tacky Peter Pantomime', a harsh appraisal, but one that acts as a reminder that *Peter Pan* had always been associated with Christmas, and by extension, in Britain, with pantomime tradition. The emergence of the play adapted to pantomime in the final decades of the twentieth century had, therefore, something to do with stage history, but this was also informed by the changing place of pantomime in British theatrical culture. *Peter Pan* as pantomime is not seen in the West End of London, where this seasonal entertainment had ceased – with very few exceptions – by the 1980s.[10] Therefore, *Peter Pan* as pantomime is seen in the regions and the London suburbs and this, combined with historical distance from the early stage history of the play, allows pantomime versions to be judged as distinct entities. Marketing will often assert that this is the traditional and familiar way to access the story; for example at the Theatre Royal, Nottingham, for the 2018–2019 pantomime season:

> With amazing flying effects, barrels of laughter, magic and fairy dust, join Peter and the lost boys and set sail in the ultimate pirate pantomime adventure complete with

> all of the ingredients audiences know to expect in this swashbuckling festive treat.[11]

Alongside this shift to pantomime, the source play has been seen in productions which proclaim themselves to be faithful adaptations, but work to represent more contemporary concerns and attitudes. Since the 1982 RSC production cast an actor, Miles Anderson, as Peter, this kind of adaptation has often placed particular emphasis upon explorations of gender and identity, with an adult male representing the boy who resists maturity, and the female characters afforded greater authority within the play world.[12] For example, the 2016 co-production by the Bristol OldVic and the NT doubled Mrs. Darling and Hook, explicitly presenting Peter's animosity towards mothers as a key motivation in his resistance to maturity. The now dominant convention in casting Peter was confirmed by *Peter Pan Goes Wrong* (2015, first produced in 2013), the metatheatrical farce from Mischief Theatre where an incompetent drama society is staging the play *Peter Pan*. Two actors take on the role of Peter as the production unfolds, and the character of Chris the director proclaims 'This is not a pantomime', as the performance taking place around him becomes increasingly shambolic.[13] The declaration insists that *Peter Pan Goes Wrong* is a homage to the Barrie source; by the second decade of the twenty-first century, that source is most often staged with an actor as Peter, so here actors try (and fail) to present the character in their disastrous production.

Screen adaptations

The developing convention of casting an actor as Peter has also been influenced by the history of *Peter Pan* on screen where, most often, boys or men have been seen in the role. One notable exception is the silent film *Peter Pan* (1924), where Betty Bronson played the part. This was initially to be based on a scenario written by Barrie, drawing on elements from the play and from *Peter and Wendy*. The scenario was eventually disregarded by director Herbert Brenon, but it remains a helpful document when assessing how film was thought, by the dramatist, to be an asset to his play. Barrie recognises that a film version would allow for a particular kind of spectacle in adaptation, and that an opening scene with Peter flying in Never Land could 'show at once that film can do things for Peter Pan which the ordinary stage cannot do. It should strike a note of wonder in the first picture, and whet the appetite for marvels'.[14]

One innovation seen in this film is the use of an actress, Virginia Browne Faire, rather than a lighting effect to depict Tinker Bell. A scaled-down image of Faire was placed on screen to present the fairy character. Subsequently, this choice for film has been translated back to the stage where Tinker Bell is frequently presented in human form. While stage technologies like reflecting from a mirror to depict the character as a darting light on stage and visible harnesses for flight can be dispensed with on film, other technologies can take their place to present the 'wonder' of Never Land, in turn extending what might be presented as *Peter Pan* on stage and screen in the future.

In the 1924 version, while some innovation is evident in the presentation of the supernatural, all major characters are retained and the plot mirrors that of the play, with intertitles reproducing particular lines. It was the Disney *Peter Pan* almost three decades later that explored how the narrative could be adapted more extensively for the screen, with adaptation creating a characteristic Disney piece. Henry A. Giroux has described the use of fairy tale and popular narrative by Disney as 'the ideological vehicle through which history is both rewritten and purged of its seamy side'.[15] The 'seamy side' of American history is certainly overwritten through this film adaptation; for example, First Nations characters happily sing the song 'What Made Red Man Red'. Also, as Deborah Cartmell notes, 'the youngest Darling, Michael, is given an American accent, whereas his older siblings, John and Wendy, speak the Queen's English with the implication that the pure, natural, pre-lapsarian voice is that of an American'.[16] This, and the American accent of Peter, position youth and magic as qualities to be found within America and by Americans; as with the musical produced the following year, this Peter is a 'fun-loving American boy'.[17]

While the animated film retains the narrative arc of the source play, references to mortality are omitted, and the opening scene presents a new motivation for the Darlings to join Peter, as Wendy has been told by her father she must soon leave the nursery, and the journey to Never Land provides an escape from that prospect. However, while the first minutes of the film promise to afford more agency to Wendy, the Never Land environment allows female characters to present only a limited range of behaviour. Wendy takes on the role of mother, while Tinker Bell, Tiger Lily, and the mermaids all portray aggression towards her, fuelled by their desire for closeness with Peter. It is not until the 2002 sequel, *Return to Never Land*, that the leading female character (this time Wendy's daughter Jane) is presented as a more complex and opinionated character, refusing to take on the role as mother. Yet it is the 1953 film, providing additional motivation for the children to escape to Never Land, circumventing references to the death of characters, and claiming *Peter Pan* as about an American boy, that has continued to resonate through many subsequent screen versions.

For example, in the 1991 Steven Spielberg movie *Hook* we are presented with an all-American Peter in the form of Robin Williams. Here, a grown man who has forgotten his time in Never Land must recuperate his childhood persona to save his own children from the machinations of Hook (Dustin Hoffman). Grown-up Peter is to some extent made possible by the popular Disney precursor, which confirms that Peter was indeed an American boy just a few decades earlier. The influence of the animated film conjoins with intertextual resonances from Williams' career, including *Mork and Mindy* (1978–1982), the television role that made his name, where he also portrayed a character from out of this world who displayed decidedly childish traits. *Hook* demonstrates that by the final decade of the twentieth century, *Peter Pan* was such a familiar narrative that it could be adapted to show a Peter who does not remain a boy, and to tell the story – so the title claims – from the perspective of the villainous pirate. However, in practice, the film remains quite closely linked to its source as Peter defeats Hook (again), retrieves his children from Never Land, and returns to a world where his parenting, and their maturity, can proceed. Ultimately, the American nuclear family is celebrated, as an ideal American boy was in Disney's interpretation.

It was in 2003, as a precursor to the play's centenary, that another film titled *Peter Pan* was released, directed by P. J. Hogan. This is consciously positioned as a close reworking of the Barrie narrative, but casts a young American actor (Jeremy Sumpter) as Peter, echoing yet again the Disney adaptation. The film is very much of its time, reflecting the popularity of pre-teen narratives including the early instalments of the *Harry Potter* franchise, with Peter and Wendy sharing a kiss towards the end of the film. It was marketed as a defining adaptation, with the line 'The timeless story as you've never seen it before' adorning posters. Opening during the Christmas season and reproducing the narrative arc and much of the dialogue from the published play text, the film carefully follows that source, while making space to reformulate attitudes to gender and to character motivation. The Disney film continues to permeate, as Wendy is told she must leave the nursery and incites her father's anger through childish behaviour; but the authority of this Wendy does now extend in to Never Land, where she propels much of the action. Also, the villainy of Hook is given some grounding as his fear of ageing and of loneliness are shown – through the numerous asides afforded to Jason Isaacs in his presentation of the character – to influence his behaviour. However, the insistence of this film upon its role as a faithful and consequently authoritative screen version of Barrie's narrative demonstrates a concerted effort, after a century of *Peter Pan* in performance, to market this film adaptation as a unique offering through its very adherence to the play.

Appropriating *Peter Pan*

Looking beyond adaptations, it is apparent that as a 'meta-text' the play *Peter Pan* has many offshoots. A brief examination of some allusions to and appropriations of elements in the play will demonstrate its enduring presence and influence, and the uses to which it has been put. For example it is worth acknowledging the material value ascribed to Peter Pan, the character who has become, in the words of Maria Tatar, 'a figure divorced from the original stories'.[18] This phenomenon is satirised in the period drama *Mad Men*, where a botched 1960s advertising campaign for 'Peter Pan's Tinkerbell's cookies' is featured in the episode 'The Forecast'. By turning the iconic characters in to a brand, the episode demonstrates the countless ways that *Peter Pan* was being disseminated by the middle of the twentieth century; it both critiques the appropriation of these characters and acknowledges that similar processes are still at work, making the *Mad Men* storyline legible.

Not all appropriation is as covert and fleeting, of course. For example, *Finding Neverland* (2004) clearly incorporates and reworks the play *Peter Pan* and the process of its composition. While the film is acknowledged to depart significantly from what is known of Barrie's life, it does represent the complex range of experiences that influenced his work. So, for example, a relationship between Barrie and the Llewellyn Davies family is depicted, but the father to the boys, Arthur Llewellyn Davies, has died before Johnny Depp's Barrie encounters the rest of the family, while the five young brothers become four. These details contest the historical record but allow for a clear narrative that emphasises the role of imaginative play in the development of *Peter Pan*, as Barrie spends an increasing amount of time amusing the boys and befriending Sylvia Llewellyn Davies at the expense of his already strained marriage. Rather than aiming to bring a complex, intimate, and ultimately unknown series of interpersonal relationships to the screen, the film creates a coherent story by reformulating some of the contextual factors that are known to have influenced composition of *Peter Pan*. *Finding Neverland* coincided with the centenary for the play's first production and so, like Hogan's 2003 film, it was read as a response to the status of the play after a century of production and adaptation. Both films use CGI technology to represent the Never Land realm, utilising twenty-first century processes to do what Barrie implied would be valuable in reworking his text for the screen, to 'strike a note of wonder'.

Finding Neverland also provides a fruitful example of how, after a century, it is impossible for those adapting the source play to prevent the history of *Peter Pan* in performance from seeping in to their work. Intertextual references populate the film; for example, Charles Frohman is played by Dustin Hoffman, his role as the title character in Spielberg's *Hook* ghosting the performance. Yet in *Finding Neverland* it is the controlling and rigid mother of Sylvia Llewellyn Davies who is presented as an initial model for Hook, and so the presence of Hoffman subtly undermines the tale of the play's composition that is being presented. Another intertextual marker, but one that endorses the story being told, is the presence of Depp as J.M. Barrie. When a reviewer in *The Telegraph* commented in 1906 that 'Mr. Barrie has done no better work than by the creation of this quintessence of all piratical villains',[19] the influence of Hook upon subsequent depictions of the pirate could not be foreseen. The character certainly feeds in to the amoral dandy Jack Sparrow as played by Depp in the *Pirates of the Caribbean* franchise, a character first presented to audiences one year before the release of *Finding Neverland*. However, Peter also permeates the Sparrow persona. For a knowing audience, that ornithological surname and the familiarity of the character with supernatural realms would invite comparison:

> HOOK 'Tis some fiend fighting me! Pan, who and what art thou?
>
> (*The children listen eagerly for the answer, none quite so eagerly as Wendy*)
>
> PETER (*at a venture*) I'm youth, I'm joy, I'm a little bird that has broken out of the egg.[20]

Once alerted to these parallels, other similarities between the characters become apparent; most notably, Peter Pan and Jack Sparrow both refuse to show concern with the essential constraints of mortality and time that circumscribe the actions of others. Therefore, in *Finding Neverland* Depp as Barrie not only presents a story of how the play came in to being, but evokes an association that emphasises the influence of *Peter Pan* in mainstream cinema, subtly promoting the value of a film about the play's origins.

There are other recent examples of work recognising and meditating upon the influence of *Peter Pan*, including the presence of some of its content in the television series *Once Upon A Time* (2011–2018). The show reformulates narratives and characters from fairy tale and children's literature, and this kind of drama relies upon, in the words of Jeff Casey, 'a sort of intertextual dissonance between itself and its antecedent texts', so that a source, in this case *Peter Pan*, becomes a point of comparison. The very disruption of audience expectations aims to grab and to hold the attention of that audience; for example, in the series, Peter brutalises vulnerable youngsters rather than making them part of his community.[21] The 2015 film *Pan* employs a similar approach, providing an origin story for Peter in a 1940s London ravaged by the blitz, before showing us how he becomes the Peter Pan of Never Land. This disrupts preconceptions, taking Peter out of the Edwardian age, and the film goes on to consistently play with expected narrative. Here, James Hook is an all-American adventurer in the Indiana Jones mould and an ally for Peter, while the villain is Blackbeard (Hugh Jackman), who retains the '*dandiacal*' costuming expected of Hook but survives by means not of piracy, but of heavy industry. He abducts boys and men to mine fairy dust on the island of Never Land, is introduced on screen to a rendition of Nirvana's 'Smells Like Teen Spirit' chanted by his workers, and tellingly rails to his crew that 'there is no time'. Within the world of this film, the line refers to his urgent need for fairy dust, a substance that promises eternal youth, but in relation to this as one among many versions of *Peter Pan*, the line also suggests what we are to take from a prequel set four decades after composition of the play. Peter can have his origins in the 1940s, but that does not mean he cannot visit the Edwardian nursery of the Darling children, or indeed the Seattle grunge scene of the 1990s. By 2015 *Peter Pan* has been produced and read for more than a century and in *Pan*, points of reference from across the period are used to create a Never Land made out of mainstream cultures that have lived with the play as inspiration since 1904.

Notes

1 Peter Hollindale, 'A Hundred Years of Peter Pan', *Children's Literature in Education*, 36:3 (2005), 197–215, pp. 197–198.
2 Sarah Cardwell, *Adaptation Revisited: Television and the Classic Novel* (Manchester: Manchester University Press, 2002), p. 25.
3 Barrie, *Peter Pan*, Act 1, p. 98.
4 'Gaiety Theatre', *Times*, 24 December 1927.
5 *Times* review, 24 December 1949, quoted in Hanson, *Peter Pan on Stage and Screen*, p. 264.
6 Michael Quinn, 'Celebrity and the Semiotics of Acting', *New Theatre Quarterly*, 6:22 (1990), 154–161, p. 155.
7 Margherita Laera, 'Introduction: Return, Rewrite, Repeat: The Theatricality of Adaptation' in *Theatre and Adaptation: Return, Rewrite, Repeat*, ed. by Margherita Laera (London: Bloomsbury, 2014), pp. 1–18 (p. 2).
8 Quoted in Christopher Lucas, 'The Tale of Two Peters: Broadway Hail Mary Martin', *Daily Mirror*, 22 October 1954.

9 Further details of the changes made to the source play for the 1954 musical can be found in Teresa Jones, 'Peter and Me (or How I Learned to Fly)', in *Second Star to the Right*, pp. 243–263.

10 *Aladdin* at the Old Vic in 2004 and 2005 is one, unusual instance of pantomime returning to West End and central London venues.

11 Theatre Royal, Nottingham, https://trch.co.uk/whats-on/peter-pan-2/ [accessed 9th May 2018].

12 One rare early example was in 1952 in Germany, when Eric Kästner's translation of the play was produced with an actor in the role of Peter.

13 Henry Lewis, Jonathan Sayer, and Henry Shields, *Peter Pan Goes Wrong*, 3rd edn (London: Bloomsbury, 2015), Act 1, p. 34.

14 J.M. Barrie, 'Scenario for a Film of Peter Pan', quoted in Green, *Fifty Years of 'Peter Pan'*, p. 172.

15 Henry A. Giroux, quoted in Deborah Cartmell and Imelda Whelehan, '"To Die Would be an Awfully Big Adventure": The Enigmatic Timelessness of Peter Pan's Adaptations', *Cadernos de Tradução*, 1:7 (2001), pp. 93–107 (pp. 97–98).

16 Deborah Cartmell, 'Adapting Children's Literature', in *The Cambridge Companion to Literature on Screen*, ed. by Deborah Cartmell and Imelda Whelehan (Cambridge: Cambridge University Press, 2007), pp. 167–180 (p. 171).

17 Quoted in Lucas, 'The Tale of Two Peters'.

18 Quoted in Vincent Dowd, 'Why Did Theatre Turn Its Back on Original Peter Pan?', *BBC World Service*, 16 December 2013, www.bbc.co.uk/news/entertainment-arts-25333685 [accessed 7th May 2018].

19 'Peter Pan: The Third Year', *The Telegraph*, 19 December 1906.

20 Barrie, *Peter Pan*, Act 5, Scene 1, p. 146.

21 Jeff Casey, 'Queer Cannibals and Deviant Detectives: Subversion and Homosocial Desire in NBC's Hannibal', *Quarterly Review of Film and Video*, 32 (2015), 550–567, p. 554.

Conclusion

Peter Pan is now presented to us in many forms. Some adaptations proclaim an affinity to J. M. Barrie's *Peter Pan*, typically combining elements from the 1928 play text with subsequent prose versions, most notably *Peter and Wendy*. There are many subtler appropriations of the text, treating it as a flexible 'meta-text', imported to connote meaning within a quite different production. This book has been concerned with the play and its presence on stage and screen since 1904, with a particular focus upon a kind of trans-Atlantic evolution. *Peter Pan* has of course been reworked in other cultural contexts and in other forms including the graphic novel and the digital realm of gaming. Although not alone in achieving notoriety as a piece of drama well suited to various processes of adaptation, the play holds a very particular status as a product, initially, of imaginative play, which remains particularly malleable. So, while the copyright status maintained in consideration of Great Ormond Street Hospital exercises some control over use of the source text, the pervasive nature of *Peter Pan* through both adaptation and more subtle intertextual allusion is sustained and prominent.

Never a play only for or about children, *Peter Pan* continues to emerge from a vast range of texts and performances, speaking to and about diverse audiences. As a final example, it is evident in Jez Butterworth's state of the nation play *Jerusalem* that the protagonist Rooster Byron shares qualities with the character one reviewer of the 2009 play defined as 'another seditious outlaw who headed a gang of misfits: Peter Pan'.[1] Rooster, inhabiting an England devastated by the march of suburbia, full of tall tales fostered by substance abuse, and visited by the lost boys and girls of rural Wiltshire, is in Ben Brantley's words, 'a poisoned Peter Pan'.[2] Even the name recalls the characteristic 'crowing' of Peter in his victories over Hook. *Jerusalem* presents a stage world where Peter Pan grows up, and his Never Land is diminished by adult priorities as the council seeks to move him out of the way of a property development. While many audiences will want to see a younger, less sordid, more reassuring depiction, it is worth noting that the character first moulded by Barrie, the Llewellyn Davies boys, and numerous theatre practitioners saw every experience including death as an adventure. Surely, Peter himself would revel in the complex, varied, and often surprising cultural afterlives of *Peter Pan*.

Notes

1 Paul Taylor, 'Jerusalem, Apollo Theatre, London', *Independent*, 11 February 2010. The parallels to Peter Pan were exacerbated in the first London and New York productions by the casting of Mark Rylance as Rooster Byron. Rylance had played Peter in an RSC production of *Peter Pan* in 1983.

2 Ben Brantley, 'This Blessed Plot, This Trailer, This England', *The New York Times*, 11 April 2011.

Filmography

Finding Neverland, dir. by Marc Forster (Miramax, 2004).
Hook, dir. by Steven Spielberg (TriStar Pictures, 1991).
Mork and Mindy, ABC, 14 September 1978–27 May 1982.
Once Upon a Time, ABC, 23 October 2011–18 May 2018.
Pan, dir. by Joe Wright (Warner Bros., 2015).
Peter Pan, dir. by Herbert Brenon (Paramount Pictures, 1924).
Peter Pan, dir. by Clyde Geronimi, Wilfred Jackson, Hamilton Luske, Jack Kinney (RKO Radio Pictures, 1953).
Peter Pan, dir. by P. J. Hogan (Columbia TriStar, 2003).
Return to Never Land, dir. by Robin Budd, Donovan Cook (Walt Disney Studios Motion Picture, 2002).
'The Forecast', *Mad Men*, Season 7, AMC, 19 April 2015.

References

'A Joyous Night with Peter Pan', *The New York Times*, 7 November 1905.

'At the House Near Strand's Top: Manager Wendy', *The Sketch*, 4 September 1912.

Barrie, J.M., *Peter Pan in Peter Pan and Other Plays*, ed. by Peter Hollindale (Oxford: Oxford University Press, 1995).

Barrie, J.M., *Peter Pan, or, the Boy Who Would Not Grow Up*, introduction by Andrew Birkin (London: The Folio Society, 1992).

Biographical File for Cissie Loftus, V&A Theatre & Performance Department.

Biographical File for Gerald du Maurier, V&A Theatre & Performance Department.

Biographical File for Hilda Trevelyan, V&A Theatre & Performance Department.

Birkin, Andrew, *J.M. Barrie and the Lost Boys*, 2nd edn (New Haven: Yale University Press, 2003).

Brantley, Ben, 'This Blessed Plot, This Trailer, This England', *The New York Times*, 11 April 2011.

Broadbent, Elizabeth, 'Peter Pan and the Roots of Racism', *Huffington Post*, 11 December 2014, www.huffingtonpost.com/elizabeth-broadbent/peter-pan-and-the-roots-o_b_6301724.html [accessed 10th May 2018].

Cardwell, Sarah, *Adaptation Revisited: Television and the Classic Novel* (Manchester: Manchester University Press, 2002).

Cartmell, Deborah, and Imelda Whelehan, '"To Die Would Be an Awfully Big Adventure": The Enigmatic Timelessness of Peter Pan's Adaptations', *Cadernos de Tradução*, 1:7 (2001), 93–107.

Cartmell, Deborah, and Imelda Whelehan, eds., *The Cambridge Companion to Literature on Screen* (Cambridge: Cambridge University Press, 2007).

Casey, Jeff, 'Queer Cannibals and Deviant Detectives: Subversion and Homosocial Desire in NBC's Hannibal', *Quarterly Review of Film and Video*, 32 (2015), 550–567.

Dowd, Vincent, 'Why Did Theatre Turn Its Back on Original Peter Pan?', *BBC World Service*, 16 December 2013, www.bbc.co.uk/news/entertainment-arts-25333685 [accessed 7th May 2018].

du Maurier, Daphne, *Gerald: A Portrait* (London: Gollancz, 1934).

'Duke of York's Theatre', *Times*, 28 December 1904.

'Entr'Actes No. 27; Gerald du Maurier', *Daily Sketch*, 2 December 1932.

'Fiscal Policy and the Commonwealth', *Times*, 29 September 1904.

'Gaiety Theatre', *Times*, 24 December 1927.

Hammerton, J.A., *J.M. Barrie and His Books* (London: Horace Marshall, 1900).

Hanson, Bruce K., *Peter Pan on Stage and Screen 1904–2010*, 2nd edn (Jefferson, NC: McFarland & Company, 2011).

Hollindale, Peter, 'A Hundred Years of Peter Pan', *Children's Literature in Education*, 36:3 (2005), 197–215.

Innes, Christopher, *Modern British Drama: The Twentieth Century* (Cambridge: Cambridge University Press, 2002).

Jack, R.D.S., 'Barrie as Journeyman-Dramatist: A Study of Walker, London', *Studies in Scottish Literature*, 22:1 (1987), 60–77.

Kavey, Allison B., and Lester D. Friedman, eds., *Second Star to the Right: Peter Pan in the Popular Imagination* (New Brunswick: Rutgers University Press, 2009).

Laera, Margherita, ed., *Theatre and Adaptation: Return, Rewrite, Repeat* (London: Bloomsbury, 2014).

Lancelyn Green, Roger, *Fifty Years of 'Peter Pan'* (London: Peter Davies, 1954).

Lane, Anthony, 'Lost Boys: Why J.M. Barrie Created Peter Pan', *The New Yorker*, 22 November 2004.

Lewis, Henry, Jonathan Sayer, and Henry Shields, *Peter Pan Goes Wrong*, 3rd edn (London: Bloomsbury, 2015).

Lowe, Shirley, 'Peter Pan Still Refuses to Grow Up', *Daily Express*, 12 December 1953.

Lucas, Christopher, 'The Tale of Two Peters: Broadway Hail Mary Martin', *Daily Mirror*, 22 October 1954.

Marcosson, Isaac F., and Daniel Frohman, *Charles Frohman: Manager and Man* (London: John Lane, 1916).

Mavor, Carol, *Reading Boyishly: Roland Barthes, J.M. Barrie, Jacques Henri Lartigue, Marcel Proust, and D.W. Winnicott* (Durham, NC: Duke University Press, 2007).

Meynell, Viola, ed., *Letters of J.M. Barrie* (London: Peter Davies, 1942).

Morley, Sheridan, 'Daphne du Maurier Evokes Her Father, Sir Gerald, the Last of the Great Edwardian Actor-Managers', *The Listener*, 9 August 1973.

'Mr. Barrie's New Play', *Edinburgh Evening News*, 28 December 1904.

'Mr. Barrie's New Play: A Real Children's Pantomime', *Manchester Courier and Lancashire General Advertiser*, 28 December 1904.

National Theatre, www.nationaltheatre.org.uk/shows/peter-pan [accessed 16th April 2018].

'New Novels', *The Graphic*, 12 May 1888.

Olssen, Michael R., 'All the World's a Stage: The Information Practices and Sense-Making of Theatre Professionals', *Libri*, 60 (2010), 241–252.

'Our London Letter', *Aberdeen Daily Journal*, 28 December 1904.

'Peter Pan at the Duke of York's Theatre', *The Manchester Guardian*, 28 December 1904.

'Peter Pan: The Third Year', *The Telegraph*, 19 December 1906.

Production File for Peter Pan, Duke of York's Theatre, 1904, V&A Theatre & Performance Department.

Quinn, Michael, 'Celebrity and the Semiotics of Acting', *New Theatre Quarterly*, 6:22 (1990), 154–161.

Rochelson, Meri-Jane, 'Language, Gender, and Ethnic Anxiety in Zangwill's Children of the Ghetto', *English Literature in Transition 1880–1920*, 31:4 (1988), 399–412.

Rose, Jacqueline, *The Case of 'Peter Pan', or the Impossibility of Children's Fiction* (Philadelphia: University of Pennsylvania Press, 1992).

Schwartz, Michael, *Broadway and Corporate Capitalism: The Rise of the Professional-Managerial Class, 1900–1920* (New York: Palgrave Macmillan, 2009).

Stirling, Kirsten, *Peter Pan's Shadows in the Literary Imagination* (New York: Routledge, 2012).

Taylor, Millie, *British Pantomime Performance* (Bristol: Intellect Books, 2007).

Taylor, Paul, 'Jerusalem, Apollo Theatre, London', *The Independent*, 11 February 2010.

'The Playhouses', *Illustrated London News*, 7 January 1905.

'The Story Behind the Story of Peter Pan', *Daily Mail*, 17 December 1964.

Theatre Royal, Nottingham, https://trch.co.uk/whats-on/peter-pan-2/ [accessed 9th May 2018].

Vanbrugh, Irene, *To Tell My Story* (London: Hutchinson, 1948).

'Vaudeville Theatre', *Times*, 19 December 1901.

White, Donna R., and C. Anita Tarr, eds., *J.M. Barrie's 'Peter Pan' In and Out of Time* (Lanham, MD: Scarecrow Press, 2006).

'"Why Fear Death?" Say Heroes of the Sea', *The Ogden Standard*, 19 June 1915.

Index